From Dinham Mill to G

the story of Cyril Lello
– a craftsman footballer

By
Barbara Ridgway

Published by Scenesetters

Publishers: Scenesetters, Ash-Leys, Bucknell, Shropshire, SY7 0AL Tel: (01547) 530660.

ISBN: 1 874200 11 4

Printed by: Welshpool Printing Group, Welshpool.

Illustration credits:
Photographs and other illustrations, except where otherwise indicated, are taken from the collections of the author or of the Lello family. Permission to reproduce copyright material has kindly been given by the following: Sheelagh Lewis, p. 24, Michael Powis, p. 27, Shropshire Weekly Newspapers, pp. 29, 38, 68, Everton FC, front cover and pp. 40, 42, 43, 50, 53, Liverpool Daily Post & Echo, pp. 44, 45. Every effort has been made to trace other copyright holders and apologies are extended to any copyright holders whose rights have been unwittingly infringed.

Contents

Preface and acknowledgements 6
Foreword by Dave Hickson 9

1. Introduction 10
2. Growing up at Dinham Mill 12
3. A footballing teenager .20
4. A footballing airman 32
5. A professional footballer – the Everton years 39
6. A veteran footballer 56
7. A footballer in retirement 61
8. Reflections 65

Bibliography 70
Index 72

Preface and acknowledgements

Cyril Lello had heroic status in Ludlow when I was a child, and the sad news of his death in 1997 prompted me to think that there should be some kind of memorial in the town to one of its most eminent twentieth century sons. Some time later I began to collect material, thinking that it might develop into a modest display in the town's museum, but the sources were so copious and of such interest that the scheme developed into a book. I hope that the book is worthy of Cyril Lello's memory, and that it will be of interest, not just to Ludlovians, but to all who follow football, and particularly to those who support the clubs for whom Cyril Lello played.

Many people have provided material for the book. First and foremost Cyril's family, his brother Harold and his late sister-in-law Joan in Ludlow, and his son Cyril Francis in Liverpool, have been wholly supportive, and generous in giving me access to material and in hospitality. I must also record my thanks to Cyril's nephew Don Smout, and to other members of his family in Ludlow.

I have been fortunate in being able to talk with several of Cyril's childhood and teenage friends. I am particularly grateful to Bill and Esmée Nash, who provided not just information and hospitality but a succession of valuable contacts. The recollections of Jack Reynolds of Shaw, Lancashire, and the late Alf Pilson of Poole, Dorset, have been particularly important. Bill and Marg Badlan and the late Ben Nicholas of Ludlow also provided some valuable memories. I am also grateful to Sheelagh Lewis for transcribing some of the recollections of her late father, Les Small, founder of Ludford Amateurs FC.

Terry Tyler of Grays, Essex, has given me a marvellously detailed description of his encounters with Cyril Lello, when he was a schoolboy in the mid-1950s, and I must also record my gratitude to BBC Radio Essex who enabled me to make contact with Terry.

I have also been able to establish links with some of Cyril Lello's wartime colleagues, and would like to record my thanks to Jack and Jean Brunton of Silsden, Ted Daines of Norwich and Joe Morris of Cambridge, as well as to Air Mail, the journal of the Royal Air Force Association, and to Donald Harris and Jim Penny for their advice on matters relating to the RAF. Peter Duckers of the Shropshire Regimental Museum kindly provided information on the military career of Cyril Lello's father.

I must also record my thanks to Don Everall, Mike Heath, Arthur Hughes and Sam Rogers, who came into contact with Cyril when he was playing football in the post-war period. It has also been a privilege to hear the memories from that period of Frank and Mary Griffin.

Many people from Ludlow have provided valuable information and leads, amongst them Colin and Rachel Badlan, John Carter, Madge Cartwright, Mary Cooper, Ronnie Dahn, Mary Davies, Stanley Hiles, Bill Jeffs, Joan Nash, Min Tipton, John Wheeler and Audrey Morley and Pam Gerrard, daughters of the late Superintendent E G Kershaw. I am indebted to all of them, and apologise if there are omissions from the list.

Susan Davies and Henri Quinn have assisted my research by the loan of books. John Powell and Terry Howells have contributed useful material from the library of the Ironbridge Gorge Museum. Sue Cooper and Janice Cox have given genealogical advice. John Swannick has provided invaluable assistance with photographs, and with Internet research.

I have also received valuable help from people at Cyril Lello's former football clubs, from Tommy Clinton, Dave Hickson, Alan Myers and Nicola McMahon at Everton FC, from Mike Jones, Kevin Ratcliffe, Chris Smith of the Away Supporters Club, Mike Thomas and Jamie and Charlie Tolley at

Shrewsbury Town FC, and from Barbara Evans, Ellen Evans, Erica and Peter Gwilliam, John Nash and Bert Torr at Ludlow Town FC. I am also grateful to those associated with Cyril's former opponents, Hookagate United FC, Bill and Michael Powis, Alan Williams, Rodney Hunter and Wilf Richards

Like all historical works this book owes much to librarians and archivists. I am particularly pleased to acknowledge the support of Ludlow Museum, where Ann Waite has been both helpful and hospitable, and to record my thanks to Tom Morris, Superintendent Registrar for the Ludlow district and to the staff of Shropshire Records and Research, Shrewsbury Reference Library, Hereford City Library, the Ironbridge Gorge Museum, Lincoln City Library, the Norfolk Studies Centre at Norwich, Rochdale Local Studies Library and Runcorn Library and Wolverhampton Archives.

Finally, I am grateful to my husband, Barrie, for his advice, encouragement and support.

Barbara Ridgway
Shrewsbury
May 2001

Foreword

I have many good memories of playing alongside Cyril Lello. He was here at Goodison when I came to the club as a young player in May 1948, and we played together many times in the seven seasons that followed.

I particularly remember his contribution to the team during the 1953-54 season when we secured promotion back to the First Division. He was a hard player on the field whose tackles were not enjoyed by opponents, but he was a superb passer of the ball and created many opportunities for his forwards.

Cyril was always a gentleman off the field, and a good companion on our trips abroad. He was one of the most loyal and consistent players ever to represent Everton Football Club, and I am delighted that Barbara Ridgway has written his life story.

Dave Hickson
Goodison Park
June 2001

1. Introduction

Football in the twenty first century is associated with money and glamour. Even a short career with a leading team can enable a player to acquire a fortune large enough to absolve him from the necessity of working for the rest of his life should he be so inclined. Through the medium of television the game is hugely popular, and a pervasive topic of conversation at all levels of society. Most politicians find it expedient to claim allegiance to a particular team. It is the most international of sports, reflected not just in the World Cup or the meetings of glamorous clubs but in the close attention paid to the game in communities of all kinds in most countries of the world, in mining villages in Lorraine or Luxembourg or small towns in Calabria or the Basque Country. It excites enthusiasm equally in Africa, in South America or Scandinavia.

This is the story of Cyril Lello, a professional footballer who flourished at a time when the game was at its most popular in England, but when players received only meagre financial rewards. The highest ever total of attendances at Football League matches, more than 41 million, was achieved in the 1948-49 season, Cyril Lello's first full season in the First Division, as the excitements of the game helped to mitigate the austerity of a period when Britain was struggling to pay back the debts incurred during World War II. Football in the post-war years was illuminated by the skills of a generation of legendary players, the goalkeepers Frank Swift, Bert Trautmann and Gil Merrick, the defenders Billy Wright, Neil Franklin and Alf Ramsey, the forwards Stanley Matthews, Tom Finney, Len Shackleton and Nat Lofthouse, whose achievements remain in the memories of all who saw them play. Cyril Lello performed with distinction in this company. He shunned celebrity, but is recalled with respect by all who played with him.

Cyril Lello's story illustrates many aspects of the history of the twentieth century. He was born in 1920, part of the baby boom that followed the Great War, eleven months after his father returned from the Western Front. He himself served in the RAF for six years during World War II, often under fire, as he helped to defend airfields from attacks by the Luftwaffe. He saw the ruins of north German cities as the war came to an end, and encountered his brother on a German football field named 'Highbury' by its British occupiers. Cyril Lello's early career shows how limited were the opportunities open to young people growing up in a picture book market town in the 1930s, and how deeply local football clubs were rooted in their communities.

Cyril Lello became a professional footballer in August 1939, and after gaining footballing as well as battle experience in the RAF, returned to the game seven years later. He soon progressed to Everton, and in spite of injuries, remained with the club for nine seasons, gaining many plaudits for his skill in games in which his opponents included the most celebrated players of the time. For a time he enjoyed a life which in some respects was glamorous, but the meagre financial rewards that he gained in the era of the maximum wage dictated that he had to continue working when his First Division career was over. After an unhappy few months in the Northern Section of Division Three, he enjoyed four productive years as player-manager with a Cheshire League club, before his playing career was ended by injury when he was 41. He took a job with a Liverpool electrical firm, working there until he reached retirement age. Ironically the ending of the maximum wage created circumstances in which he was able to continuing living in the house adjacent to Everton's ground to which he had moved on his marriage in 1950.

Cyril Lello died in 1997 leaving no diary or other records of his career, other than two family scrapbooks. The reminiscences of his family, his schoolfriends, his colleagues in the RAF and his professional team mates have been used to piece together the life of a footballer who saw himself as a proud craftsman rather than a celebrity, whose career illustrates much about the history of football, about the town in which he grew up, and about the experience of living in twentieth century England.

Cyril Lello in training towards the end of his time at Everton

2. Growing up at Dinham Mill

Cyril Lello grew up in the shadow of Ludlow Castle, on the edge of one of England's most picturesque market towns. Ludlow lies nearly thirty miles south of Shrewsbury and rather more than twenty miles north of Hereford, the nearest towns of larger size. The Welsh border lies 16 miles to the west. Cyril's home stood alongside the River Teme close to the spot from which J M W Turner and countless other artists painted the castle. The view from the family home extended over Thomas Telford's Dinham Bridge towards Whitcliffe, the wooded area and common land known to the tourists from all over the world who visit the town each year as the best vantage point from which to photograph the stately parish church of St Laurence and the panoramic view of Ludlow's streets set against the backcloth of the Clee Hills. This is also the area to which generations of geologists have come to hunt for evidence of the earth's history and its earliest forms of life in the fossil beds along the banks of the River Teme.

Dinham Mill, showing Castle Mill Cottage as it was when the Lello family lived there, before the construction of the swimming pool in the early 1960's.
From an old postcard

The name Lello is unusual and always prompts conjecture about Latin or Hispanic origins. The traditional view, quoted by C W Bardsley in his standard work on surnames published in 1901 suggests that it is derived from the Italian, although T J and P Morgan's more recent work on Welsh surnames suggest that it is derived from the Welsh, Llello or Lelo. The concentration of instances of the name along the border between England and Wales in the Ludlow area suggests that the latter explanation is plausible. The latest study of the history of Ludlow notes that in 1938 there were eleven householders in the town with the name Lello, most of them not directly related to each other.

Cyril Lello's father moved to Ludlow from Herefordshire. Thomas Henry Lello migrated to the Shropshire town from the village of Pudleston east of Leominster, and found employment as a labourer and under-gardener. While living at Tinkers' Hill, in the parish of Ludford to the south of the town, he met Clara Jane (always known as Jane) Preece, who was working in Ludlow as a domestic servant. They married in Ludlow Register Office on 13 June 1908 when both were aged 20, the marriage being witnessed by James Green and Mary Ellen Preece. Jane's address was given as Lower Galdeford, and as her mother was by then widowed they probably lived with her at No 43

Lower Galdeford, a terraced house near Warrington Gardens on the eastern side of the street that was demolished in 1967 to make way for new council accommodation. There were several other, unrelated Lello families in the area, including the owners of a tannery who lived at Springfield House, and a family who kept a sweetshop at No 50.

Almost a year after the wedding, on 13 May 1909 Jane gave birth to her first child, a daughter, sadly born blind. Gertrude Ellen Lello, known as 'Nellie', was baptised at the church of St Laurence on 29 May. Two years later on 18 July 1911 a second daughter, Winifred Elsie, was born. She too was baptised at the parish church, on 3 August 1911. The first of Thomas and Jane's four sons, Stanley Edward, known as 'Ted' was born on 30 March 1914 and baptised on 15 April of that year.

The Great War began in the following summer. Thomas Lello served on the Western Front in the King's Shropshire Light Infantry and the Machine Gun Corps. Surviving records provide few details of his service, but he was evidently in France and Flanders for much of the war, and received service medals indicating that he had been involved in actual conflict. The war memorial in Ludlow lists 137 citizens of the town who did not return from the Great War. Thomas Lello was more fortunate. He was discharged from the army on 16 March 1919 and went home to Ludlow a fit man. How he had been affected psychologically by his experiences on the Western Front must remain a matter for speculation.

The family's second son, the subject of this book, was born on 24 February 1920, eleven months after his father's return from the war. He was baptised Cyril Frank at the parish church on 9 March. Thomas and Jane had two further sons, Harold George, born on 1 December and baptised on 17 December 1921, and Leslie John, born on 3 June and baptised on 16 June 1923.

A photograph taken during World War I of Lance Corporal Thomas Henry Lello of the King's Shropshire Light Infantry

After the war Thomas Lello worked for the Ludlow Electric Light Co., which had been established in 1906 and provided power for the town from a small generator operated by a Crossley gas engine in Portcullis Lane. Power from this source was supplemented by a hydro-electric power station at Dinham Mill, one of Ludlow's ancient water mills, which had housed the foundry of the Hodges family between 1822 and 1892. The hydro-electric plant at Dinham Mill was extended in 1923. Four years later the Ludlow Electric Light Co. was taken over by the town council and sold to the Shropshire, Worcestershire & Staffordshire Electric Power Co. In 1928 Thomas Lello was appointed to look after the installations at Dinham, and he moved with his family from Lower Galdeford to Castle Mill Cottage adjacent to the plant. When the Ludlow generating plants closed down he became a linesman for the SW&S, working from the company's depot on the site of the original power station in Portcullis Lane.

The Lello Family Tree

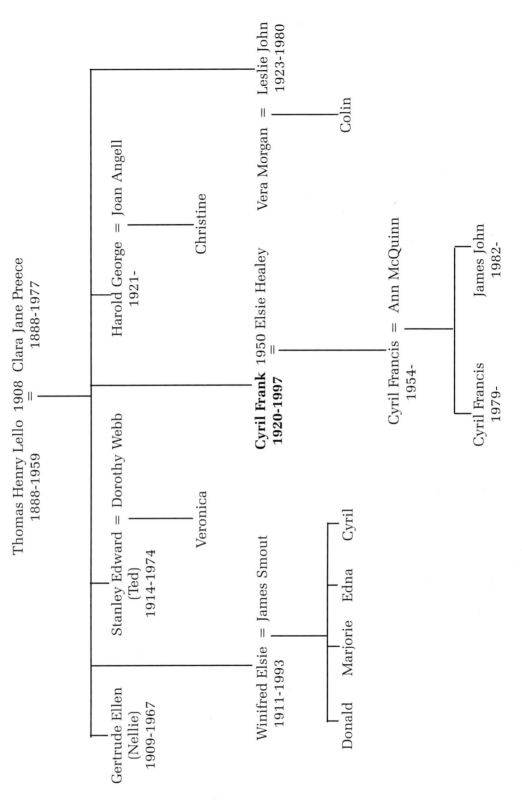

Thomas Henry Lello 1908 Clara Jane Preece
1888-1959 = 1888-1977

Gertrude Ellen
(Nellie)
1909-1967

Stanley Edward = Dorothy Webb
(Ted)
1914-1974

Veronica

Winifred Elsie = James Smout
1911-1993

Donald   Marjorie   Edna   Cyril

Harold George = Joan Angell
1921-

Christine

Cyril Frank 1950 Elsie Healey
1920-1997 =

Vera Morgan = Leslie John
1923-1980

Colin

Cyril Francis = Ann McQuinn
1954-

Cyril Francis
1979-

James John
1982-

Thomas Henry Lello standing on Dinham Weir

When the Lello family moved to Dinham, Cyril was aged eight, Harold was six and Leslie four. After the cramped terraced house which had been their first home, this was an idyllic spot for the three young brothers. Harold remembers waking early on summer mornings and looking out of their bedroom window to watch otters playing like children on the banks of the Teme. The boys fished in the mill race which flowed at the bottom of their garden just yards from the cottage door. On Sunday mornings they would cross Dinham Bridge and scramble up the steep escarpment, past the fossil beds, to play amongst the bracken on Whitcliffe, usually football, but cricket in the summer months. In winter the river sometimes flooded the garden and the ground floor of their home, but the family coped with this inconvenience, for the benefits which they enjoyed during the greater part of the year brought ample compensation. The family occasionally had difficulty in persuading Jane to leave her home when floods threatened, and Harold recalls one occasion when they had to remove his mother through the roof space to escape the rising waters.

Flood water pouring through Dinham Bridge

At summer weekends and on Bank Holidays the town and these stretches of the river banks were invaded by visitors, chiefly from Birmingham and the Black Country. On several occasions Harold pulled from the river children unaccustomed to such surroundings. He also had to discourage them from entering the mill buildings and climbing over the electrical plant, a dangerous magnet for inquisitive young minds.

As he grew older Cyril spent more of his time

playing on Whitcliffe with his younger brothers, and with his school friends Bill Nash and Alf Pilson. The friends had to be skilful, for this beauty spot was full of natural hazards. The surface sloped steeply and was broken by tussocks of coarse grass and numerous holes that were homes to rabbits and moles. There were thorn bushes and large areas of bracken to be avoided, and adders might emerge to bask in the sun on exceptionally hot days. Bill remembers a potentially serious incident when Alf Pilson fell on to a stake of freshly-cut bracken, puncturing an artery in his wrist which could have proved fatal but for the prompt action of his friends in applying pressure to the wound. A further example of this kind of comradeship occurred in May 1932 on the other side of Dinham Mill, on the Linney Field, a sports field for many generations of Ludlovians. Several youths were playing with a small ball when one of them, Leslie Angell of 18 Lower Galdeford was accidentally kicked on his right ankle. When it became clear that the injury was serious his companions carried him to the Ludlow Cottage Hospital where Dr Hunter treated him for what proved to be a broken bone in his leg.

Cyril was educated at the Ludlow National Schools, built in 1857, and situated almost opposite his first home in Lower Galdeford. When he began school at the age of five he merely had to cross the road to join the infant class, where he was taught by Miss A E Evans, a well-liked teacher who worked at the school for 26 years. He would also have been taught by the headmistress, Miss Bessie Padfield, at that time nearing the end of a long teaching career. The school was highly respected. In 1926 a report by one of His Majesty's Inspectors of Schools commended 'a continued high state of efficiency', commenting that 'these quite young children are excellently handled'. Miss Padfield retired in March 1927, about the time that Cyril moved up to the junior department of the school.

At about this time the Lello family moved to Castle Mill Cottage, which resulted in a much longer journey to school for Cyril and his brothers. After climbing the steep hill at Dinham they had the choice of two routes, either through the narrow streets of the town, or along the quieter lanes which follow the line of the ancient town wall through Camp Lane, Silk Mill Lane, St John's Road and Friar's Walk.

Cyril and his contemporaries were fortunate in their education, for during the 1920s the Shropshire County Council made increasing provision for children in their final years at school. There was a ten-year plan, instigated by A R Clegg, chairman of the Education Committee from 1922, to renew equipment and books, and to provide new accommodation. In 1926 the Hadow Report had recommended that elementary school children between the ages of 11 and 14 should be taught in separate senior schools, large enough to provide a practical education appropriate to their needs. In 1929 W H Pendlebury, the county's Secretary for Education, proposed the creation of senior schools for such children. One of the first was in

The Lello children outside Castle Mill Cottage, shortly after the family had moved from Galdeford: left to right: Cyril, Ted, Harold, Les and Winnie.

Ludlow, where the interior of the National School was re-ordered, and a new practical block constructed at the southern end of the playground. The new Senior School was opened on 2 April 1930 by the Bishop of Hereford, who observed that it was the first of its kind in his diocese.

When Cyril moved into the new school in the following year he would have worked in newly-constructed, light and airy classrooms, well-equipped with practical facilities. One was a workshop where he learned woodwork, which was to prove a lasting interest. When interviewed by a Liverpool Echo reporter at Goodison in 1955, at the peak of his career, he included woodwork amongst his hobbies, and the reporter noted *'he is greatly interested in woodwork and has made many things for the house. He is at present engaged knocking together a play pen for the son and heir. He is such a lively little fellow that he will have to be fenced in to keep him out of mischief'*.

Mr Burton, the headmaster, decided that it would be appropriate for some of his senior pupils to learn printing, and an Adana press, of a kind widely advertised in the popular newspapers of the 1930s for home use, was set up in a shed at the bottom of the school garden. It was worked by a treadle, and the type was composed by hand. Later a superior machine was installed in the main school building. In 1931 the boys began to print a school magazine called *The Broad Gate*. The first issue lists Jack Reynolds as sports editor. Jack gained an interest in printing as a result of working on the press, was subsequently apprenticed as a printer with the *Ludlow Advertiser*, and continued in the printing trade for the rest of his working life.

The girls at the Senior School enjoyed similar facilities that were designed to enable them to learn domestic skills, which they soon exercised for the benefit of the school. In November 1933 the *Ludlow Advertise*r reported that after the school football team had concluded a match with Craven Arms, the visitors were entertained to tea at The Cookery at the Senior School.

Outdoor space at the school was limited to a cramped yard. Any sporting activity took place on a 4-acre field in Sandpits Road, which had been given to the borough corporation in 1928 for use as a recreation ground for children from the town's elementary schools by James Wheeler of Bitterley Court, who had been a successful athlete at Eton and captain of the Bridgnorth rowing club. During the Second World War half the area was used as allotments in the 'Dig for Britain' campaign, and subsequently council houses were built around the edges of the field. The road running along two sides of it was named Wheeler Road commemorating the benefactor. It remains a recreation ground

The playing field in Sandpits Road showing Miss P.S.H. Perry, Headmistress of East Hamlet Junior School, with her class, in June 1949

in 2001. Children gained some exercise in the long walk from Lower Galdeford to the recreation ground, either up the steep Rock Lane, or through the town via Gravel Hill and Livesey Road.

Sport was not a priority in the school curriculum, nor was there a regular programme of matches for the school team. Occasional games were arranged against teams from nearby schools, like Craven Arms and Bitterley, but most of these were small village schools which had difficulty in finding a team of boys over eleven, and there was no real competition for the boys of the Ludlow Senior School. Bill Nash, sports editor of *The Broad Gate* wrote at Christmas 1932 that it was difficult to get matches with other schools, but that the school hoped to arrange one or two fixtures in the spring term. By contrast the elementary schools in Shrewsbury played each other on a regular basis within a school league. A regional team was selected from the best players in the town which was matched against teams from towns of similar size, notably Chester in 1933, and Wolverhampton and King's Norton in 1937, giving the boys a wider range of experience and opportunity.

When he moved from the junior department to the Senior School, football, for Cyril, ceased to be a childish pastime and became an all-consuming passion. It was the chief motivating force of his life. He played more and more, and was determined to improve his skills. Bill Nash remarked that his friend did nothing else but kick a ball up and down, and considered him 'football-mad'. He continually headed and kicked the ball against the end wall of the Castle Mill 'until he almost knocked it down'. On entering the senior school in 1931 Cyril went straight into the school team, and gave a good account of himself playing with boys two years older than he was. The older boys recognised that a precocious talent had appeared in their midst. Jack Reynolds, then in his final year at the school, and later a fellow-member of local youth teams, described him as a 'natural', in the 'top-class', who could play anywhere. If Ludlow had not been so isolated, 'in the outback' as Alf Pilson, who made his career elsewhere, expressed it, Cyril might have represented England as a schoolboy international.

It was as a schoolboy that Cyril Lello first gained fame as a footballer. In November 1933, along with Alf Pilson, he represented the school in a 7-1 victory against Craven Arms. The *Ludlow Advertiser* reported that from the centre-forward position he radiated many fine passes for his fellow forwards and was also responsible for breaking up many dangerous movements by the opposition. The family tradition was maintained after he had left school when his brother Harold was commended by the *Advertiser* for giving the best display in a 1-0 victory over Bitterley school.

At this time teachers taught most subjects rather than specialising in one or two. A favourite with both boys and girls at the Ludlow Senior School was Alan Brown. Out of school he was a keen sportsman. He played for the Ludford Amateurs football club, and was a member of the team that won league and cup honours in the 1934-35 season. He took the boys to play football and doubtless recognised and encouraged Cyril's obvious talents. During the 1937-38 season, the schoolmaster played alongside his 17-year-old former pupils, Bill Nash and Cyril Lello, and it may well have been his prompting which led the boys to sign for the club.

The three younger Lello brothers were all-round sportsmen. When asked if Cyril was good at other sports, Harold replied 'We all were'. The three boys all played cricket in summer, and in the athletics event staged as part of Ludlow's coronation celebrations in 1937 Leslie Lello won the obstacle race for boys of 12-14 years, and came second in the 100 yards. Boxing was popular amongst youngsters in Ludlow in the 1930s but the Lellos were content to watch, while their friends and footballing colleagues Jack and Artie Collier gained considerable fame as amateur boxers.

Cyril's particular friends were Bill Nash and Alf Pilson. When the three were not playing football they would often meet outside the old Picture House (now the Assembly Rooms) in the town centre, sometimes for mischief. Alf recalled 'We were young lads, what would you expect?' Cyril was a handsome young man and readily attracted girl friends, but he had more difficulty in keeping them. His first love appears to have been a maid who worked at Dr Hunter's house in Brand Lane and who came from Wistanstow. When Bill asked Cyril one day if he was still courting, he replied that she had packed him up because all he thought about was football!

Bill Nash was sports editor of *The Broad Gate*. In the sixth issue of Volume One, at Christmas 1932, he wrote '*C Lello is an outstanding player*', which, for a 12-year old critic, proved a remarkably perceptive prophecy.

FOOTBALL

Football is going as strongly as usual and a keen competitive spirit is being awakened. Every boy wishes to get into the school team and we should in time be quite able to turn out a well-balanced team It is difficult to get matches with other schools but we hope to arrange one or two fixtures. C. Lello is an outstanding player, while other good players are :- C. Carter; J. Collier; W. Hopton; C. Baker; R. Jacks; A' Edwards and G. Pritchard

The Ludlow Senior School magazine, The Broad Gate, Christmas, 1932

The Broad-Gate

The Magazine of the
Ludlow Senior Boys' School

Vol. 1. NO. 6.   XMAS 1932

SCHOOL MOTTO
[Puer Hominem Facit]

Price 2d.

Printed by the
Ludlow Senior Boys' School

Below: Form 2 at Ludlow Senior School in 1932.
Alan Brown is the teacher - back row, far right.
Bill Nash is fifth from the left in the middle row.
Cyril Lello and Alf Pilson were for some reason absent when the photograph was taken.

Above: Cyril Lello may well have taken this photograph of his great friends Bill Nash and Alf Pilson on Whitcliffe in 1937, about three years after they had left school.

3. A footballing teenager

Ludlow in the 1930s was a market town with just over 5,500 inhabitants, rather less than at the turn of the century. Most of its shops remained in private ownership, for few chain stores had been opened in the town. There were not many inviting openings for school leavers. Most of those who left the Grammar School or the High School for Girls with school certificates intent on entering the professions had to look further afield for employment. The more able male students of the Senior School might enter as apprentices the cheerful cameraderie of Ludlow's building trade, or join one of the town's family-owned shops as a boy-of-all-work and progress over the years to the position of aged and trusted retainer. Some of those with ambition sought work outside the town. Of Cyril Lello's closest friends, Bill Nash trained as a plumber, while Alf Pilson at the age of 18 went to work in the motor trade in Birmingham. Cyril, like many Ludlow teenagers, went to work at a family-owned retailing business, the greengrocery shops of the Portlock family at No 68 Broad Street and No 19 King Street. The family also had a shop in Leominster, which until his death in December 1933 was run by William Portlock whose two sons George and Gerald managed the Ludlow premises. The family's chief concern in life tended to be horses rather than the retailing of fruit and vegetables. They kept a variety of horses in fields on the eastern side of Ludlow. 'Portlock's performing pony' had a leading role in the town's coronation festivities in 1937, and the family rode to hounds, at least to Boxing Day meets of the North Ludlow Hounds at the Castle. In the *Ludlow Advertiser* in March 1949 Gerald Portlock published a well-informed article on spotting winners.

They were also keen on other field sports, and twice in the spring of 1933 William Portlock provided venison to be distributed to the needy through Ludlow's soup kitchen. Cyril may well have found them congenial employers, for his consuming interest was football rather than the pursuit of a career in greengrocery. Ben Nicholas, another keen young Ludlow sportsman, recalled that Cyril was '*all football*'. His employer ensured that when he was sent to the Sandpits area of the town it was always late in the day because if he went near to the Ludlow Town ground at the end of St Julian's Road he would probably be attracted by the football that was almost continuously in progress and fail to return to the shop.

During the 1930s the Boys' Brigade flourished in Ludlow. A unit linked with the parish church met at St Stephen's Hall, a church meeting room in a cul-de-sac off Upper Galdeford. For a while Cyril and Harold Lello were members, principally for the opportunities it provided for playing football,

PORTLOCK'S

BROAD STREET

A Special Display of selected

Fruit & Flowers

FOR EASTER.

The Best Quality, at lowest prices.

Phone 5.

An advertisement for Porlocks the greengrocers which appeared regularly in the Ludlow Advertiser in the late 1930's

rather than for religious reasons. There are few newspaper records of its activities, but on 2 March 1934 the *Ludlow Advertiser* records that Cyril Lello played in a match for the Boys' Brigade and scored a goal. Harold Lello remembers marching practices which took place in St Stephen's Hall on Friday evenings. When marching concluded and the boys were dismissed they usually contrived to leave a boy, usually one of small stature, in the space under the stage that accommodated tables and chairs when they were not in use. After a pretence at leaving the hall for home and checking that their leaders were well clear of the nearby streets, the boys returned to the hall. The door would be unlocked from the inside by the small accomplice, and they would spend the rest of the evening playing football in the hall. Electric lighting was installed in February 1934 but they would probably have been inhibited from using it by the fear of attracting the attention of nearby residents.

A range of football clubs in and around Ludlow offered opportunities to Cyril Lello and his friends as they progressed through their teens. Both Cyril and his brother Harold played for the 'Try Hards' founded by Jack Reynolds, who was two years older than Cyril and lived in Warrington Gardens, a terrace off Lower Galdeford. He probably knew the Lello brothers as young children when they lived at No 43 Lower Galdeford. He had certainly been impressed with Cyril's footballing ability at school, and recalls that he was immediately accepted as a member of the Senior School football team when he came up from the junior class, and that he excelled even when playing with boys two years older than he was.

The 'Try Hards' football team, c.1934. Back row: left to right:- Jack Adams (coach), Bill Marston, Clifford Hobbs, Jack Marston, Jack Collier, - Dodd, Cyril Lello; front row:- Alfred Pilson, Harold Lello, Jack Reynolds, Clifford Marston, Cyril Davies.

Jack Reynolds, in his mid-teens, organised the club's affairs, collecting subscriptions of a penny a week in order to pay for kit. The team was coached by Jack Adams, himself a notable local footballer who kept goal for Ludford Amateurs and Ludlow Town. The 'Try Hards' played at Oakley Park, three miles north of Ludlow, probably because Jack Adams lived in the adjacent village of Bromfield. Jack Reynolds captained the team, which included the three brothers, Bill, Clifford and Jack Marston, Jackie Collier, better known as a boxer, Clifford Hobbs and Alf Pilson, who had played with Cyril in the Ludlow Senior Boys' School team, and Cyril Davies, who later married Alf's sister, Mary. The team was completed by the two Lello brothers, and a lad named Dodd.

The few local newspapers that survive from this period record a team that was not especially successful. The *Ludlow Advertiser* on 28 December 1934 reported that Clee Hill Boys defeated the Ludlow 'Try Hards' by 6-1, and the *Shrewsbury Chronicle* on 24 April 1936 noted that they had been defeated 0-2 by Motor Club A in the first round of the Ludlow Knock-out Football Competition. The following week the *Chronicle* reported that the 'Try-Hards' had lost 2-3 to the Early Closers, but teams were not listed, and it is possible that by this time Cyril Lello was playing for the Early Closers. At the start of the following season in September 1936 the 'Try Hards' lost 2-3 in an away friendly with Craven Arms Boys Club.

The 'Try Hards' also played cricket, but the surviving newspaper reports suggest that they enjoyed no greater success. In the first round of the junior Ludlow Cricket Knock-Out Cup competition in June 1934 they were heavily defeated by the 'Blot-Outs', scoring only 55 in reply to their opponents' total of 185 for 6. The 'Blot-Outs' went on to win the competition in convincing style. The following year the 'Try Hards' were again knocked out of the Knock-Out Cup in the first round.

After he left school Cyril joined a team that was closely associated with the world of work. The Ludlow Early Closers Club was highly regarded. Most of its members worked in shops. Its matches took place on Thursdays, early closing day in Ludlow, and it was sometimes known as the Thursday Club. Matches for those employed in the retail trades were also organised in Shrewsbury, where early closing day was also on Thursday. The name of Sheffield Wednesday in Division One also recalls the association between football and early closing. The Early Closers team was managed by Jim Laver, who was rather older than the other players, and kept a newsagent's, confectioner's and tobacconist's shop at No 11 High Street. During the coronation celebrations in 1937 he employed the 16-year-old Harold Lello to sell postcards outside the Castle. Jim Laver was a leading figure in local amateur football, and was chairman of the South Shropshire League for many years. He presided over the Ludlow Charity Football Cup Committee, managing the competition and allocating the proceeds to local good causes. He also ran a dance band which played at charity functions. Those who played in the team included Jack Scott, the jeweller, whose shop was also in High Street, John Bodenham, whose family had a furniture store in Quality Square, Wilf Mapp, from Gaius Smith, the grocer's in King Street, Tony Cooper and Jack Davies, who were employed at the grocery shop of W S Stephens in Upper Galdeford, and Frank Cartwright, who worked for Sale & Higginson (later Burgesses), the agricultural merchants in Corve Street. Other members were Frank Acton, Ernie Arrowsmith from Clee Hill, Bradney Banks, Deany Burton, George Clark, 'Bandy' Freeman, Harold Lello, Wally Powell, the three brothers Dennis, Gordon and Jack Tipton, and a man called Williamson who played in goal. The membership of the team covered all social classes, from the sons of wealthy jewellers to mere errand boys like Cyril.

In December 1932 the *Ludlow Standard* reported that the Ludlow Early Closers had 'a wonderfully good record to their credit, having given fine displays in three successive away matches, a 2-2 draw, and 4-0 and 5-2 wins'. Sportsmen were asked to uphold the sporting traditions of Ludlow by supporting members of the team who had given good service to their shops over the Christmas period.

The Early Closers played in the Ludlow Thursday League, the Ludlow Thursday Cup, which they won in 1034, the Ludlow Knock-out Cup in which they were runners-up in the same year, and the Ludlow Charity Cup competitions. In the 1034-35 season they gave a good account of themselves in the Hereford Thursday League, in which they gained a creditable 3-3 draw with Ledbury in mid-January. The performance of their inside-right was particularly commended, and while he is not

The Ludlow Early Closers team in c 1936. Most of the team worked in shops in Ludlow. It is significant that Cyril Lello, although far from being the oldest member, occupies the captain's position.
Back row: left to right:- Mr Bithell (referee), Jack Scott, Wilf Mapp, Ernie Arrowsmith, Jim Laver, John Bodenham, unknown (possibly - Martin from Clee Hill), Bill Nason; front row: left to right:- Bradney Banks, Harold Lello, Cyril Lello, Wally Powell, Frank Acton.

named in the report it was almost certainly Cyril Lello, who was to celebrate his 16th birthday on 24 February 1935, and who appeared in team photographs published in the *Shrewsbury Chronicle* in May 1934, February 1936 and April 1937. The Ludlow Early Closers also played in the Shrewsbury Thursday Cup and Amateur Challenge Competition, but were not admitted to the Shrewsbury Thursday League until September 1935 because of the travelling distance for Shrewsbury-based teams

The Early Closers team played well during the 1935-36 season. In April 1936 they beat Ludlow Motor Club B 7-1 in the first round of the Ludlow Knock-out Competition, and gained a 3-2 victory against the 'Try-Hards in the semi-final. In May they beat Ludlow Town 3-2 to win the competition. In February 1936 and April 1937 they played charity matches in Ludlow against teams representing Shropshire Police, winning the latter 6-4.

As Cyril grew older his appetite for football increased. In the 1937-38 season he found a place in the Ludford Amateurs team, perhaps as a result of the prompting of Alan Brown, his former schoolmaster. The club had been founded in 1922 by Edward Leslie (Les) Small, then 17 years of age, to provide himself with a worthwhile interest after he had suffered two close family bereavements. Like Jack Reynolds in the following decade he carried considerable responsibility in the club while still in his teens. Les Small subsequently became a successful farmer at the Riddings,

where he established a prosperous dairy business, and at Foldgate. He played at outside-right with Ludford Amateurs until 1935. He died at the age of 95 while this book was being researched. Les persuaded his father to hold an inaugural meeting in the billiard room of the family home at Sheet Farm. A committee was formed which consisted of his father, Ben Small, Mr C T Davies who farmed at Huck's Barn, a Mr Jones, a local tailor, who kept a shop later known as Harveys, Mr Boulton, who was appointed secretary, and Mr Bill Robbins who agreed to take on the post of treasurer. About a dozen younger men of Les's age attended the meeting. A black and white strip was adopted, and the first match was played in a field that belonged to the Small family's farm, on the site of the present roundabout where Sheet Road crosses the A49 by-pass.

Les Small, founder of Ludford Amateurs, taken in the early 1990s. Inset: Les Small as a footballer in the early 1930s.

Initially Ludford Amateurs played in the North Herefordshire League, along with Ludlow Town and most of the teams from nearby villages. In the 1934-35 season both Ludford Amateurs and Ludlow Town were playing in the southern section of the South Shropshire League. Ludford Amateurs enjoyed a spell of considerable success in the mid-1930s. Over the Easter Holiday period of 1932 they won the finals of both the Church Stretton Nurse Cup and the Leintwardine Cup. In the 1934-35 season they were champions of the South Shropshire League and won the Knowbury Nurse Cup. They had to scratch from a cup game

The Ludford Amateurs football team c. 1926.
Back row: left to right:- Joe Lloyd, -, Len Steel, Tom Davies, W Jackson, Mr Howells, - Charlton, H Sheldon; middle row: left to right:- C Davies, W Jones, V Cheadle; front row: left to right:- Jack Potts, C Jones, L Williams, H Badlan, L Small.

at Craven Arms in January 1935 because they were engaged in so many other competitions. They asserted their supremacy over the much older Ludlow Town club by beating them 6-0 in a cup match in December 1934 and 6-1 in the following month. Rivalry continued in subsequent seasons. On Christmas Eve 1937 Ludford Amateurs gained a 4-3 victory over Ludlow Town in a cup game, but the older club won 7-1 in a league match on Christmas Day. By this time the 17-year-old Cyril Lello was appearing regularly at centre-forward in the Ludford Amateurs team and 'some good work by Lello' was commended by the *Shrewsbury Chronicle* in a report of a match in January 1938.

The Ludford Amateurs team 1931-32. Back row: left to right- Bill Robbins, Ted Howells, Tom Davies (chairman), - Robinson, C Davies (Hucks Barn); third row: left to right:- H Brownhill (groundsman), G Keyse, Bill Davies, H Badlan, John French, Bill Childs (trainer); second row: left to right:- Les Small, Jack Yates, Charlie Taylor, 'Togger' Davies, Wallace Pearce, Fred Parsons; front row: left to right:- Dennis Jones, 'Red-un' Pearce.

In March 1938 Cyril Lello was given a trial with Hereford United who were then playing in the Birmingham League. He played well at centre-forward in a match against Bangor City, and travelled with the club's first team as reserve for an away game against Oswestry Town. It was probably for this game that, as Bill Nash recalls, he was picked up by a Hereford United bus opposite the Feathers Hotel in Ludlow. His friends watched as he waited for the coach, boots in hand. Hereford United were in the midst of a bad run of results. They had not won in the Birmingham League since 11 December 1937, and urgently needed an effective striker. It appears that they secured the services of a Torquay United centre-forward called Keeling, and after attending a home match against Stafford Rangers on 19 March as reserve, Cyril returned to Ludford Amateurs.

The Feathers Hotel, Ludlow.

Ludford Amateurs in 1935 shortly before Cyril Lello joined the club.
Back row: left to right:- Roberts, Bill (Spud) Matthews, Wyley Jackson, George Pinches, Alan Brown, - Williams, - Campbell, Bill Everall, - Marshall, Leonard Davies, Sid Edwards, Gordon Williams, Ben Nicholas, - Cartwright; front row: left to right:- Charlie Taylor, Bradney Banks, Bill (Sooty) Pratt, Percy Dyer, Bill Burland, Paddy Oakes, Alfie Banks, Bill Childs (trainer).

Cyril scored two goals for Ludford Amateurs in a 4-1 victory in a South Shropshire League match against Clun early in April 1938. Later in the month his team met Hookagate United, in the final of the Church Stretton Infirmary Cup. The first match was drawn, but Ludford Amateurs won the replay 3-1. Cyril scored with a powerful shot, and from the re-start went straight through the opposition to score again, completing his hat-trick with a penalty not long before the final whistle. In this game he played alongside his school friend Bill Nash and their former schoolmaster Alan Brown. The following week Ludford Amateurs again visited Stretton for a cup final, in this case the Church Stretton Nurse Cup, but on this occasion were beaten 3-1 by Church Stretton FC, Cyril Lello scoring their only goal. Their league form in the 1937-38 season had been less good, and they finished the season second from bottom of the South Shropshire League, with 10 points from 16 games, while Ludlow Town topped the table.

A Hookagate United team of the late 1930s with their trophies.
Back row: left to right:- Ted Key (Royal Oak), Ellis Vow (Swan), Charlie Titley, Eric Titley, Bill Powis, 'Curly' Richards (trainer), Bob Hunter (New Inn), Arthur Seabury, supporter; middle row: left to right:- A Tudor (supporter), Jack Powis, Fred Tudor, Len 'Froggie' Richards, - Gough, Alfred 'Mutton' Richards, Hugo Cooper, Henry 'Civil' Davies, D Parry (supporter); front row: left to right:- Arthur Richards, Arthur Disley, Arthur Powis, Charlie Powis.

The rivalry in cup competitions between Ludford Amateurs and Hookagate United was deep-seated. On Easter Saturday 1932 the Amateurs had beaten Hookagate 2-1 to win the Church Stretton Nurse Cup, at a time when their opponents headed the Shrewsbury & District League. In April 1937 some months before Cyril joined them, Ludford Amateurs again beat Hookagate in the final of the same competition. Hookagate is a straggling village on the old road from Shrewsbury to Bishop's Castle. It originated as a coal-mining community, and had three pubs in the 1930s. The team was established at the turn of the century. Its traditional headquarters was and remains in 2001 at the New Inn, kept in the 1930s by Bob Hunter. Their ground was then a field on the opposite side of the Rea Brook, and their changing room was a hut that still stands in the garden of the New Inn. The Hookagate club had many successes. They were champions of the Shrewsbury & District League in 1930-31, 1931-32, 1932-33 and 1938-39, when they scored 103 goals in 22 matches, and won numerous cup competitions. The team included several groups of brothers, three Titleys, Eric, Charlie and John, three Richardses, Arthur, Len (Froggie) and Alfred (Mutton), and four Powises, Arthur, Bill, Charlie and Jack. Bill Powis, who still lives in Hookagate in 2001, has clear recollections of Cyril Lello, as a fine player, even when he was with Ludford Amateurs.

The following season Cyril changed his allegiance and began to play in cup matches for Ludlow Town, although from the start of the season in August 1938 he was also making increasingly frequent appearances as an amateur for Shrewsbury Town Reserves, which appears to have kept him out of Ludlow Town's league games. Ludlow Town were the senior local club, although in the late 1930s Ludford Amateurs were playing at the same level. According to Jasper Edwards, who served for a long spell as secretary, the club originated in 1883, and certainly in 1885 a team representing Ludlow played a game against Knighton. Football in the town was boosted around 1900 by the presence of navvies building the aqueduct taking drinking water from the Elan Valley to Birmingham. After the aqueduct was completed a meeting was held bringing together some of the clubs for whom the navvies had played, and representatives of church-based teams, both Anglican and Nonconformist. In 1937 it was suggested that a merger between Ludlow Town and Ludford Amateurs would bring a higher standard of football to the town, but Jasper Edwards argued that the existence of the two clubs provided more opportunities for local players, and that aspiring to play at a higher level

88-year-old Bill Powis, a member of the Hookagate United team of the late 1930s, who clearly remembers playing against Cyril Lello, proudly displaying his football trophies in the garden of his cottage at Hookagate in the summer of 2000.
Inset: Bill Powis as a footballer in 1938.

would lead the club into debt. Cyril Lello scored twice for Ludlow Town in a 4-1 victory over Hopton Swifts in a cup match in late November, another goal being contributed by his schoolfriend Alf Pilson. Cyril was reported to be in outstandingly good form in a 4-1 win against Craven Arms in December, scoring two goals in the first five minutes, and completing his hat-trick with the final goal of the game. The report on this match is one of the few of this period to list a Ludlow Town team, and reveals that at least nine of their players were, like Cyril, former members of the 'Try-Hards' and Early Closers. Cyril Lello scored both goals in a 2-1 victory, against Clee Hill, again in a cup competition, later in December. On 21 January 1939 he led the forward line from the inside-right position in a 4-1 cup victory against Hanwood Colliery and scored a goal. Another was contributed by Alf Pilson, and the other two by his slightly older friend Ben Nicholas, although the newspaper commented that the latter did not extend himself on account of a leg injury. The same three players played particularly well in a 3-2 cup victory against Bucknell in February.

Above: The Ludlow Town team in 1937 shortly before Cyril Lello began to play for them. Jasper Edwards, secretary of the club, wrote a letter detailing its history which appeared in the Shrewsbury Chronicle on 22 January 1937.
Back row: left to right:- J Tipton, F Milbourne, S Yapp; middle row: left to right:-
L Watkins, H Cresswell, J Gough, G Clarke, J Martin, D Tipton, G Cooper, L Davies,
C Cadwallader, Jasper Edwards (secretary), G Tipton; front row: left to right: -
G Reading, J Collier, A Collier, J Houseman, R Marsh; kneeling at the front, left:
Ken Edwards. The other two boys are - Gazey and - Marsh.

Right: Ben Nicholas at the age of 85, proudly holds his footballing trophies in the garden of his cottage alongside the River Teme. Inset: Ben Nicholas at the age of 20.

While playing for Shrewsbury Town in the early months of 1939 Cyril renewed his acquaintance with the Powis brothers from Hookagate. Arthur and Jack Powis played in a succession of reserve team matches. Bill Powis also had one game for Shrewsbury Town Reserves for which he recalls that he was paid 7s 6d. On 22 April in a reserve match at Kidderminster Arthur Powis was playing at right half, Cyril Lello as outside right and Jack Powis at outside-left. In a reserve match against Oswestry Town on 29 April Cyril scored two goals, one from a corner taken by Arthur Powis, who also contributed a goal of his own to a 5-1 victory. Both were subsequently included in the first team for a 3-2 away win against Boston United, when the Shrewsbury Chronicle praised the club's initiative in giving opportunities to promising young players. Jack Powis, the youngest of the brothers, is remembered as a particularly talented player who would probably have succeeded as a professional but for his untimely death while on military service.

Shrewsbury Town had been impressed with Cyril's contributions to their reserve team, and in late March 1939 he made his debut in the first team in a Midland League game. He played at least three more games for the first team before the end of the season, and in August 1939 he signed professional forms for the club. He played for the reserves against Worcester City reserves in the last week of August in which he scored his first two professional goals for the town. He had no further opportunity to play as a professional in the first team before the outbreak of war against Germany.

Most football clubs in the area organised social functions which took place throughout the winter months. In December 1933 the *Ludlow Standard* reported that there had been a good attendance at a dance organised by the Early Closers Football Club in the Nelson Room at the Angel Hotel, where the music was provided by Jim Laver's 'Four Aces Harmony Band' in which Cyril Lello's elder brother Ted played trombone. In March 1936 there was a combined Whist Drive and Dance at St Stephen's Hall at which Wilfred Parsonage, the well-known local bookmaker and race horse owner, was MC for the whist drive and Sam Leach, for the dance. Similar events were regularly held in St Stephen's Hall, at least one of which, in April 1937, was attended by 200 whist players.

Birmingham League

AWAY POINTS WELL EARNED
SHREWSBURY'S FORWARDS TOOK THEIR SHOOTING BOOTS!

REVO SPORTS 3. SHREWSBURY R. 6

Revo Sports, newcomers to the Birmingham League, entertained Shrewsbury Res. at Brierley Hill on Saturday in the Keyes Cup Competition. Shrewsbury made changes, trying Bartley at right-half and Davies, a recognised half-back, in the forward line.

Revo Sports: Hadley; Stanley, Lovell; Morris, Cherrington, Watkins; Collins, Taylor, Green, Beckley, Clayton

Shrewsbury Res.: Sambrook; Hardon, Seymour; Bartley, Smith, Wassall; Lewis, Davies, Lello, Powell, Hallman.

Referee: Mr. H. Whitehouse (Wolverhampton).

Revo opened strongly, three quick at-

defence could not cope with the fast open attacks of two strong wingers. From successive centres from either wing, LELLO added two more goals in four minutes, thus completing his "hat trick."

Later Revo hit back, and they had a great chance of scoring when Green went through, but he shot hurriedly, and the ball went straight into Sambrook's hands. Half-time: Revo Sports

LELLO

Perhaps the first press portrait of Cyril Lello published in the Wellington Journal of 3 March 1939 recording Shrewsbury Town's 6-3 victory over Revo Sports on 25 February 1939 and the part he played in it

Ludford Amateurs organised rather more ambitious occasions. One of the main social events in the Ludlow social calendar was the club's annual whist drive and dance, held each November in the town hall, the town's most capacious venue. In 1933 when music was provided by Fred Lawton's dance band from Shifnal, a newspaper commented that it was 'a fixture that was more largely attended as year succeeds year'. Les Small recalled that the helpers who took charge of the whist tables all wore evening dress. At subsequent dances pride was taken that music was provided by bands well-known on the radio. In 1937 the principal prize in the raffle was a football autographed by the Wolverhampton Wanderers team.

Football was closely bound up with other community activities. Cup competitions raised considerable sums of money for charities. In Ludlow itself Jim Laver's Charity Football Cup Committee provided help for many good causes. The Early Closers and other Ludlow teams competed in 'nurse cups' at Bucknell, Church Stretton, Craven Arms, Doddington, Knighton, Knowbury, Lydbury North and Presteign, each of which raised money to sustain the work of a peripatetic nurse in the locality. In April 1938 Cyril Lello was a member of the Ludford Amateurs team who were runners-up in the Church Stretton Nurse Cup. It was reported at the presentation that the nurse whose work was supported by the competition had paid 5,400 visits in the previous year. In April 1939 it was announced that the Bishop's Castle Charity Cup competition had raised over a thousand pounds for local hospitals since its inauguration in 1900.

The medal awarded to members of the team that won the Church Stretton Infirmary Cup.

With the outbreak of war at the beginning of September 1939 normal competitive football ceased. On 21 October 1939 a network of regional competitions commenced, bringing together Football League clubs with the leading non-league teams. All the competing clubs were able to call on the services of 'guest' players, full-time footballers in the armed forces who might be based in the locality. The Chief Constable published directions concerning football matches, principally that matches should be timed so that spectators could return home before sunset, and that air raid warnings must be audible on grounds. Members of the forces in uniform were admitted to Shrewsbury Town's home games at half price. The contracts of professional footballers were terminated in September, but clubs retained their registrations.

The *Shrewsbury Chronicle* in mid-September looked forward to the high standard of football that the war promised to bring to the Gay Meadow, and Shrewsbury Town soon found themselves confronting teams that, at least nominally, represented Football League clubs. Cyril Lello continued for some weeks to play at centre-forward. He scored one goal and made another in a 3-0 victory against Port Vale on 16 September, but Shrewsbury were completely outclassed when they came up against Coventry City a week later and suffered a 0-6 defeat. On 8 October they met another Football League team, Nottingham Forest, and were worthy 4-3 winners on a heavy pitch, the local newspaper commenting that the crowd were 'highly delighted with Lello'. Shrewsbury Town also included Cyril Lello in two further games against League clubs, a 0-5 defeat by West Bromwich Albion and a 1-1 draw with Preston North End.

From mid-November, for reasons that are not evident, Cyril Lello began to play for Hereford United, the club who had given him a short-lived trial in March of the previous year. Under wartime conditions the Birmingham League club had opportunities to play against leading Football League clubs, and even teams representing less illustrious clubs might include seasoned professional players as 'guests'.

Cyril's first appearance for Hereford United in 1939 was on 11 November when he played at inside-left in a 5-3 victory against Gloucester City, during which he made two goals. The following week he 'played a very constructive game' and scored his first goal for the club in a 7-0 win against Barry Town. On 9 December he played in what was billed as Hereford's 'match of the season' against Birmingham City, who, somewhat incongruously, included several Aston Villa players in their team, and were accompanied to Hereford by a celebrity in Midlands football, E A (Terry) Eden, secretary of the Birmingham County FA, well-known for his role in the BBC radio programme 'Sport in the

Midlands'. Hereford's audacity made for an entertaining game which ended in a 2-3 defeat, although the *Hereford Times* reported that 'Lello sent the crowd into ecstasies by regaining United's lead...coolly and cleverly dribbling the ball into the net'. Cyril also took part and scored a goal in a return friendly match the following week, which resulted in a 2-1 victory for Hereford.

In the early months of 1940 Hereford United's programme was much disrupted by the weather, which not only made playing conditions difficult but prevented 'guest' players from travelling from their bases to the ground. The River Wye was frozen over in early February. A home game against Cheltenham Town in late January was reduced to 35 minutes each way, and Ron Starling, the Sheffield Wednesday centre-forward who had been due to play for Hereford was unable to reach the ground. Nevertheless Hereford gained a 6-1 victory. Increasingly Cyril Lello was playing alongside and meeting with opponents who were experienced Football League players. He was a member of the team which played against Yeovil Town on 6 February that also included Ron Starling, Eric Houghton of Aston Villa and Keenan of Everton. While Starling was in the team Cyril played several games at outside-right with some success, driving in 'one of his characteristic smashers' in a game against Cardiff City. On Good Friday he came up against another well-known player, when Hereford met Worcester City for whom Frank Broome of Aston Villa was a 'guest'. Even when the team included hardened professionals it was the 19-year old Lello who took Hereford's penalty kicks, from which he invariably scored. On 16 March he returned to the Gay Meadow to represent Hereford United against a Shrewsbury Town team whose centre-forward was Jack Rowley of Manchester United, whom Cyril was to encounter on many other occasions in the course of his career.

Another footballer who was later to play an influential part in Cyril's career was active in the Hereford area in the early months of 1940. Cliff Britton, the Everton half-back, was a PT instructor in the army, based at Monmouth, and put much energy into the organisation of football matches in the Borderland. An army match took place at Edgar Street on 30 March, when Hereford United were without a game, but whether Britton was involved is uncertain. It would have been a curious irony if he had met Cyril Lello at that stage in his career. Britton was soon to become, with Stan Cullis and Joe Mercer, a regular member of the England half-back line for wartime internationals, and a decade later, as manager of Everton, he was to set Cyril Lello's career in a new direction.

On 6 April Cyril was joined by his brother Harold, regarded as 'an inside-forward of promise' for a long coach trip to play against Yeovil Town on their notorious sloping pitch. Harold recalls that running up the slope was like trying to play football on Clee Hill. Both brothers played well, and the *Hereford Times* reported: *'Lello (minor) was in the picture with a good effort and his shot struck the foot of the upright. Lello (major) met the ball and shot hard and true so that the goalkeeper who stopped it could not hold it, but it was luckily cleared by a back.....Lello (minor) has some clever touches and when he has filled out (he is only in his teens) he should make a very useful player'.* Harold played alongside Cyril in several other games during April, for one of which a Bradford City player cycled all the way from Llandrindod Wells to Edgar Street to play at left-half for Hereford.

The season concluded before the end of April just as German troops were massing for their offensive in Belgium and France which was launched on 10 May. Hereford United acknowledged when they sent a list of their registered players to the Football Association that Cyril Lello was registered with another club (i.e. with Shrewsbury Town) and that he could not be retained. The German offensive led to the evacuation of the British army from Dunkirk. The nation was entering a period of crisis. On 18 June Cyril Lello enlisted in the Royal Air Force. His experiences with Shrewsbury Town and Hereford United enabled him to declare, doubtless with pride, that his civilian occupation was 'professional footballer'.

4. A Footballing Airman

For Cyril Lello's generation the war changed everything. Young Ludlovians who might have expected to leave the town only for occasional visits to Shrewsbury or Hereford, or for a few days' seaside holiday at Borth, found themselves travelling in uniform to parts of the world known only from school geography lessons, and mastering skills which they had never expected to have the opportunity to learn.

The experiences of those who played football alongside Cyril varied widely. His brother Harold, two years his junior, was a fitter with a squadron flying Typhoon fighter bombers as part of 123 Wing of the allied Tactical Air Force. His squadron was one of the first to fly from an airfield in France. Harold landed in Normandy with other ground staff some days after D-Day, while the beaches were still under aerial attack from the Luftwaffe. The ramp of their landing craft went down into a bomb crater which meant that he and his companions had to wade ashore with water up to their armpits. Harold's squadron contributed to the destruction of German armoured forces in the Falaise pocket, and followed the British Second Army across France into Belgium and the Netherlands and ultimately into northern Germany. Cyril's other brother, Leslie, rose to the rank of sergeant in a tank regiment which took part in the Battle of Alamein, crossed the Mediterranean to Sicily and fought its way through Italy.

Cyril's two great friends also served in the forces. Alf Pilson who had left Ludlow before the war to work in Birmingham and then in Manchester, joined the RAF in February 1941. He trained at a gunnery school in Dorset, where he met his wife, before going to the Far East in 1943, serving in India and Burma. He recalled that the best time of the war for him was when he was working at a base in Assam with USAAF transport squadrons flying 'everything you could mention' into China. Bill Nash joined the Royal Engineers, and while at the Engineers' base at Chatham, met and in 1942 married his wife, Esmée, daughter of a naval family who lived locally. While she remained in Chatham, he went to North Africa and like Les Lello was part of the Eighth Army under Field Marshall Sir Harold Alexander which made its way doggedly northwards through Italy from 1943-45. Bill Nash's elder half-brother Ben Nicholas, who played with Cyril Lello for Ludford Amateurs, joined the Royal Navy and served on the sloop *HMS Black Swan* when she was escorting convoys to Murmansk. He was on board when she took a direct hit from a German bomb which mercifully failed to explode. Bill's wife Esmée was working in a naval laundry at Chatham when she heard that *Black Swan* was coming into the dockyard, and wrote to Ben's wife suggesting, without breaching security, that it would be in her interests to come to stay at Chatham. She accepted the invitation and stayed for a fortnight seeing Ben every day.

After 1945 while Cyril prospered as a professional footballer his demobilised contemporaries returned to the amateur game in and around Ludlow. Bill Nash with his half-brother Ben Nicholas, played for Woofferton where they are seen in this photograph before a Tenbury Cup match.

Billy Nason, who was a member of the Ludlow Early Closers when Cyril was their principal striker, served with the Loyal Regiment in the Middle East and represented the First Infantry Division at football, replacing Newcastle United's goalkeeper in the Divisional team. Billy Jeffs who also played alongside Cyril Lello joined the RAF, and appeared as a guest player for Coventry City, before returning home to play as centre-half and captain of Ludlow Town. His brother, Harvey Jeffs, a contemporary of Harold Lello, was a sergeant in the London Scottish and landed with his regiment on the Anzio beaches in southern Italy. Bill Badlan, later to captain the Dolphins cricket team for which Cyril made guest appearances, was a wireless operator in the RAF, searching for Japanese submarines from Catalina flying boats in the Indian Ocean. Of Cyril's other contemporaries, Jackie Collier served in the KSLI, Ben Crump in the Royal Welch Fusiliers, and John Bodenham in the Royal Artillery. All but Alf Pilson, who settled near his wife's home in Dorset, returned to Ludlow, most of them to play for Ludlow Town while Cyril was pursuing his professional career. Not all were so fortunate. Ludlow's war memorial records that 38 men from the town failed to return from the war. One of them was George Pritchard, a fellow member with Cyril of the football team at Ludlow Senior Boys' School. He was an artilleryman when he was captured by the Japanese at Singapore in 1942. His death was not officially confirmed until the summer of 1946. Jack Powis, Cyril's opponent in cup finals with Hookagate United and a fellow member of Shrewsbury Town teams in 1939, was tragically killed in a motor cycle accident in Germany near the end of the war, while serving as a signaller in the Herefordshire Regiment.

Cyril himself joined the Royal Air Force on 18 June 1940, when he was given the number 1054325. It was recorded that he was 5ft. 7 5/8 in. tall, with a 34fi inch chest, hazel eyes and a fair complexion. Tracing his RAF career has proved difficult. He underwent basic training at Blackpool, after which it appears that he followed the trade of gunner. He was one of the 29,000 ground gunners trained by the RAF between the establishment of the Directorate of Ground Defence formed at the Air Ministry on 27 May 1940 and the end of the year, following the destruction of many RAF aircraft on their

LAC Cyril Lello at home on leave during World War II.

runways during the German offensive in Belgium and northern France launched on 10 May 1940. By April 1941 the RAF had formed 150 ground defence squadrons. The need for even more effective defence of airfields was demonstrated by the campaign in Crete in May 1941, and on 8 January 1942 the war cabinet sanctioned the formation of the Royal Air Force Regiment, incorporating the existing ground defence squadrons. The new regiment wore khaki battledress with blue insignia and shoulder tabs, and from 1943 blue berets. The regimental depot was established at Belton Park near Grantham, ancestral home of Lord Brownlow, while its principal training school moved to the holiday camp at Filey, North Yorkshire. Billy Butlin had begun to build the camp before the war, but it was completed at government expense and used by the RAF Regiment until August 1945. The new Regiment demanded much higher standards of physical fitness than had been usual in the ground defence squadrons, and a post-war recruiting leaflet proclaimed 'sport is strongly encouraged in the regiment', something which doubtless appealed to the young Cyril Lello, who rose to the rank of Leading Aircraftman. He was trained to fire the 40mm. Bofors gun, the weapon that senior officers in the RAF had wanted to deploy for airfield defence in the 1930s, but which only became available in 1943, the year when a note of good conduct was inscribed on Cyril's record.

Cyril Lello's footballing activities between 1941 and 1945 provide more information about his whereabouts than his official RAF records. A series of regional competitions between professional football clubs, replacing the existing leagues, was inaugurated from 21 October 1939, and servicemen were able to 'guest' for clubs in the vicinity of their bases. In consequence footballers of humble origin had opportunities to match their talents against some of the best-known players of the time who might be turning out for relatively obscure teams.

From August 1940 and through the Battle of Britain Cyril Lello was with a ground defence squadron guarding RAF Stanbridge, an important radio transmitting station near Leighton Buzzard. Joe Morris, who served with him, also aspired to be a professional footballer, and had been a triallist with Stoke City. Joe recalls playing alongside Cyril for the station football team which included professionals from Middlesbrough, Reading and Falkirk. The officer in charge was the Arsenal and England full-back Eddie Hapgood, with whom Cyril later played in a few games for Shrewsbury Town in 1947.

By the end of 1940 Cyril was serving at Horsham St Faiths near Norwich, now the city's airport. One of his fellow servicemen, Ted Daines, recalls that he was a quiet and unassuming but always friendly character. Horsham St Faiths was in the front line of air warfare. Ted Daines recalls 7 April 1941 when eight Bristol Blenheims of 139 Squadron attacked the steelworks at Ijmuiden in the Netherlands. One was shot down and six of the rest were damaged when they returned after being intercepted by German fighters. Ted Daines was on duty alongside Cyril Lello when the damaged planes arrived back, two of them on fire, and in the evening when the Luftwaffe attacked the airfield with incendiary bombs.

Cyril played football for Horsham St Faiths against other bases in the region, and began his career as an RAF guest footballer at Norwich City. In spite of the strong RAF and Army presence in Norfolk, Norwich City sometimes found it difficult to raise teams, and the day before their defeat in the Cup by West Ham United on 13 February their projected XI included 'A Goalkeeper' and 'A N Other' at outside-left. Cyril was one of three 'RAF strangers' who were included in the Norwich City team which lost 2-3 to Southend United on 29 March 1941, at Chelmsford, which was the Southend home ground during the war. The *Eastern Daily Press* noted that the inside-left had gained professional experience with Shrewsbury Town, and was impressed by his ball control, his accurate passes and his powerful shooting, which produced a goal. On Easter Saturday he was one of a depleted team which lost 1-7 in an away fixture at Watford, but on Bank Holiday Monday played in a home victory against Luton Town. He also represented Norwich City in home League games on the following two Saturdays, creating a favourable impression with the press in both games. The game against Southend on 3 May was the last League fixture of the season, but Cyril represented the Canaries in three subsequent matches, a friendly against a strong United Services XI at Ipswich in aid of a Suffolk charity, a 9-1 home victory against a police team in which he scored a goal and deserved to score more, and an encounter with a strong RAF XI in aid of the Norfolk & Norwich Hospital and the RAF Welfare Fund on 22 May. This was the end of his two month spell at Carrow Road. He seems to have disappeared from Norfolk by the time the next season began in August 1941, and there are no indications that he played for any professional club during that season.

By the summer of 1942 Cyril Lello was probably in Northern Ireland where there were ground defence (from January 1942 RAF Regiment) squadrons based at Ballykelly, Ballyherbert, Long Kesh and Newtonards. Cyril played regularly during the 1942-43 season for Derry City in the Northern Regional League, the Irish League having been suspended for the duration of the war. The club's historian remarked that many of Derry City's servicemen guests were very ordinary players, but that a few, like Cyril Lello, were 'excellent acquisitions'. Cyril netted 20 goals for Derry City in the 1942-43 season, during which he was their highest scorer, and he achieved the only international honour of his career when he played for the North of Ireland in a friendly against the Football Association of Ireland.

Cyril's best-known achievements as a guest player were with Lincoln City in the 1943-44 season, when he was stationed at Coningsby, the celebrated Bomber Command base which now accommodates the Battle of Britain Memorial Flight. His first appearance at Sincil Bank was against Mansfield Town on 30 October 1943 when he played at centre-forward, opening the score after half an hour with what the local newspaper described as 'a low, fast, all-the-way winner, inches from the ground', the first of four goals which contributed to a 7-2 victory for the home team. The reporter appeared to think that he was an Irishman, referring to him as 'this boy from Derry City', but was impressed with the ability of 'this sprightly, opportunity-snapping centre-forward', and was certain that the crowd would want to see him again. In total he played 14 times in league and cup competitions for Lincoln City between October 1943 and February 1944, and scored 21 goals, an astonishing record. Grimsby Town on 6 November detailed several players to man-mark him, which created opportunities for his fellow players, and when he slipped his markers he scored a fine solo goal, running from mid-field to round the goalkeeper, and help his side to a 4-0 victory. He contributed two goals to a 5-1 win over Rotherham on 29 November, and netted a penalty in a 1-1 draw with Nottingham Forest on 6 December.

Cyril scored a first-half hat-trick against Notts County on 18 December, and ended the game with seven of the eight goals scored by Lincoln in an 8-5 victory. There were high scores in many wartime games, and Cyril's tally of seven goals in a game was not unique. Jack Rowley of Manchester United scored eight for Wolves in an 8-1 victory over Derby County on 21 Nov 1942, while Billy Hullett, also of Manchester United, scored seven in an away game for Lincoln City. Nevertheless the seven goals impressed the football correspondents of the national press. Harold Lello remembers looking across a barrack room and seeing a national newspaper headline proclaiming that one footballer had scored seven goals in a match, only realising that it was his brother Cyril when it was his turn to read the report.

Cyril Lello continued to play well for Lincoln City in the first weeks of 1944. He scored twice in an exciting match on 10 January before a crowd of 5,556 when Lincoln lost 4-5 to Doncaster Rovers. While he usually played at centre-forward, on 31 January at Grimsby he was Lincoln City's inside-left. He returned to the central role for a match with Sheffield United at Brammall Lane on 5 February, and scored a goal, although Lincoln lost the game 2-6. He was named for the match against Rotherham United on 26 February, but did not appear, probably because he had moved from Coningsby to another base. Many units travelled to new quarters in the early months of 1944 as the forces prepared for the invasion of France.

What Cyril Lello was doing in the spring and summer of 1944 is not known, but by mid-November of that year he was back in Lincolnshire, playing at centre-forward for Lincoln City in their 2-2 draw with Nottingham Forest on 18 November. He played again on the day before Christmas Eve against Doncaster Rovers, but thereafter disappeared from Lincolnshire for many months, although he was to make one more appearance for Lincoln City, at inside-right in a 1-4 defeat by Gateshead on 13 October 1945. He also played twice for Millwall in the 1944-45 season, although details are not currently to hand.

By the end of the war in Europe in the first week of May 1945 Cyril was with an RAF Regiment squadron at Celle in northern Germany, one of the four principal RAF bases in occupied Germany whose personnel were later to play a distinguished role in the Berlin Airlift. Joe Morris recalls that he played alongside Cyril in a team representing the RAF against the Army, while they were both stationed at Celle. Cyril's brother Harold, by this time with his Typhoon squadron at Wunstorf, received a letter from home telling him that Cyril was also in Germany. The two brothers were unable to make contact until they both ran on to the field in the final of an RAF cup competition on a ground near Hanover that had been nicknamed 'Highbury'. Harold, representing 123 Wing, did not know that Cyril was playing, until he appeared with an RAF Regiment team, which included several Wolves professionals. Harold left the ground with his brother in an RAF Regiment truck. A few weeks later Cyril took a jeep to visit Harold on precisely the same afternoon that Harold borrowed a jeep to drive to Celle. The brothers did not meet that day and must have passed on the autobahn.

Further details of Cyril Lello's activities in 1945-46 are unknown. He was photographed in an RAF football team at Haverfordwest, probably in 1945 or 1946. The players' home towns are listed on the back of the surviving print. One of them, Jack Brunton, still lives at Silsden near Keighley, but he does not recall the occasion. Cyril Lello was demobilised on 15 July 1946, when he returned to live with his parents at Castle Mill Cottage. A full programme of League football was due to resume in August, and Joe McClelland, secretary-manager of Lincoln City, for whom he had played so well in wartime, was anxious to secure his services. At a spirited meeting of supporters in the last week of August 1946 there were demands from the floor that Lello be signed, and the chairman replied that the transfer would take place as soon as the club had permission to make the necessary approach. Such permission was not forthcoming, and Shrewsbury Town, for whom he had not played for seven years insisted on retaining his registration. Lincoln City signed many new players on the eve of the season, but Cyril Lello was not amongst them.

Above left: An RAF football team at Haverfordwest, probably just after the end of World War II. Cyril Lello occupies the captain's position in the centre of the front row. The team is listed on the reverse. J R Brunton (middle row, extreme right), still lives in Silsden, just outside Keighley, but cannot recall the occasion.

Above right: The reverse of the Haverfordwest photograph, showing the names and home towns of the team.

Cyril Lello in his 'demob' suit in the summer of 1946.

Shrewsbury Town were then in the Midland League, and had been champions in the 1945-46 season, but in the absence of automatic promotion and relegation, did not achieve League status until 1950. The Gay Meadow spectators, like those at Sincil Bank and Carrow Road, had seen unprecedented numbers of distinguished players in the course of the war. The Shropshire Senior Cup Final against Wellington Town on Easter Monday 1944 included players from Wolverhampton Wanders, Birmingham City, Chelsea, Tottenham Hotspur, Manchester City, Partick Thistle and Celtic, and the game was refereed by a regimental sergeant major. In November 1944 a game of American football was played at the Gay Meadow. There was already a sense in Shrewsbury in August 1946 that Cyril Lello was a very special player. The *Shrewsbury Chronicle* heralded his appearance in the club's public practice match and, in the second week of the season, reported on his achievements with Lincoln City. Cyril continued to live with his parents in Ludlow, but from time to time, when returning late from an away match would spend the night at lodgings in Shrewsbury. In the summer months he was employed by the club as an assistant groundsman.

The season began well for Shrewsbury, with Cyril amongst the scorers in a 6-3 victory against Bradford City Reserves in the opening match on 31 August. Three days later he scored twice in a 4-1 victory over Boston United. He scored 25 goals in the Midland League in the course of the season, and five in the Welsh Cup. For the first two months of the season he played at inside-right, but moved to inside-left from mid-November, although he returned to his original position for two games towards the end of the season, and twice on 19 October 1946 and 5 April 1947 played at centre-forward. A highlight of the season was an 8-1 defeat of Denaby United on 13 December 1946 during which he scored another of his memorable solo goals. Games during the early months of 1947 were severely disrupted by frost and snow. A move which demonstrated Cyril's ability to trick his opponents was one of the few memorable features of a 2-1 victory over Scarborough amid ice and snow on 7 February. He scored twice in a 5-0 defeat of Peterborough United on 22 February, which only went ahead because several inches of snow had been removed from the pitch. The ice and snow were followed by floods, and the last Midland League game of the season was not played until 31 May when Cyril scored twice in a 4-0 victory at Newark against Ransomes & Marles, which left Shrewsbury Town in sixth place. He also scored in a 3-1 victory in the final of the Shropshire Senior Cup against Wellington Town at the Buck's Head on 7 June 1947, and with other members of the team received a pint tankard in recognition of their success. Wellington Town, as losers, received half-pint tankards.

Below: The pint tankard won by Cyril Lello as a member of the Shrewsbury Town team who beat Wellington Town to win the Shropshire Senior Cup in June 1947.

Shrewsbury Town Team. There are newcomers in the Shrewsbury Town football team this season. Our picture, taken on the Gay Meadow on Saturday, shows (seated) Lello, S. Hughes (capt), Pringle and Butler; (standing) Mr. T. Seymour (trainer), A. Hughes, Maxwell, Wheatley, Streten, Sykes Rogers, Owen and Aldred.

Cyril's regular companion during his only full season as a professional with Shrewsbury Town was Arthur Hughes, a one-time miner from Hanwood, whom he had encountered playing for Pontesbury in amateur football before the war. Arthur had also served in the RAF, and like Cyril, was demobilised in the summer of 1946. They trained together and sat together on the team coach. Arthur remembers that when they first met at the Gay Meadow, after six years away from football in Shropshire, they recalled cup games in which they had been opponents. He regarded Cyril as the outstanding player in the Shrewsbury team, although he was modest about his abilities, and shunned ostentatious goal celebrations.

Shrewsbury Town's Midland League opponents included the reserve teams of 11 League clubs, whose managers would certainly have observed Cyril's ability to make and score goals. Nevertheless Shrewsbury were themselves ambitious, and applied for the sixth time in the summer of 1947 for admission to the Northern Section of the Third Division. Evidence of the club's intentions was provided by their securing the services of the veteran ex-Arsenal and England full-back Eddie Hapgood, who signed in August 1947.

The new season began well for the club. They won their first match, lost the second, but then won eight and drew one of the next nine. Cyril Lello, who had a slight injury, missed the opening game against Bradford Park Avenue Reserves, but played well in matches against Denaby, Lincoln, Scarborough and Grantham. The latter was an away fixture on 11 September 1947, from which the club coach returned too late for Cyril to catch the last train back to Ludlow. He stayed the night in lodgings after what was to prove his final game for Shrewsbury Town.

Arthur Hughes aged 83 in 2001

5: A professional footballer: the Everton years

On Friday 12 September 1947, the day after his late return from Grantham, Cyril Lello was instructed at the Gay Meadow to get into a car with Shrewsbury Town officials. About ten miles north of Shrewsbury, as the car sped across the north Shropshire plain, Leslie Knighton, the manager, told him that they were on their way to Goodison Park where he was to sign for Everton. Cyril's parents had expected him home for lunch, and were concerned when he did not appear.

The affairs of the Merseyside club were then in the hands of a secretary-manager, Theo Kelly, whose son, it was rumoured, had heard of Cyril's footballing prowess during the war. There seems no evidence for this link. It is more likely that his success with Shrewsbury Town had drawn him to the attention of several League clubs, and certainly Wolverhampton Wanderers appear to have been disappointed that such a skilled player from within what they regarded as their territory had been snatched from them. W R Williams, the Everton chairman, had apparently watched Lello play for Shrewsbury on several occasions before deciding to sign him. The transfer fee was not revealed. Newspapers reported it variously as 'several hundred pounds', a 'four-figure fee' or £2,000. Leslie Knighton, said that the fee was 'highly satisfactory for Shrewsbury' but that the club were more concerned to advance Lello's career than to make money. It was rumoured that Theo Kelly tried to avoid revealing Cyril's age – he was 27 when the transfer took place and 28 when he made his first team debut the following year – and for several years newspaper reports referred to him, rather pointedly as a 'youngster'.

Everton were amongst the aristocrats of the First Division. They were founder-members of the Football League and had been champions twice in the 1930s, when their record of success was second only to that of Arsenal. The club had been weakened by the sale of two of their most celebrated players. Tommy Lawton, one of the greatest of English-centre forwards, went to Chelsea in November 1945, and Joe Mercer, left-half and captain of England left Merseyside for Arsenal in December 1946. The club finished tenth in Division One at the end of the 1946-47 season. By the summer of 1947 only five players, Norman Greenhalgh, Tommy Jones, Ted Sagar, Alex Stevenson and Gordon Watson remained of those who had won the championship eight years earlier. The policy of Theo Kelly and the directors was to seek for talent in Ireland, where they obtained the services of Tommy Eglington and Peter Farrell from Shamrock Rovers. They also scoured the lower divisions of the Football League for players who would strengthen their team, which was how they came to obtain the services of Cyril Lello.

Cyril's debut for his new club was auspicious. He played at inside-left for Everton's reserve team in a Central League fixture with Wolverhampton Wanderers reserves at Molyneux in the afternoon of Monday 15 September. Everton won the game 3-1. Cyril scored Everton's first goal in the 55th minute and provided the passes from which Harry Catterick, manager of the club in the years of their success in the late 1960s, scored the other two. Nevertheless it was more than five months before Cyril appeared in the first team. Everton played Wolves four times in the 1947-48 season. On 4 October 1947 Alex Stevenson, Peter Farrell and Tommy Eglington were all playing for Ireland, and before the FA Cup-tie on 24 January 1948 Peter Farrell broke his jaw, but Lello appeared on neither occasion, nor did he take part in the subsequent replay. Nevertheless it was again against Wolves and again at Molyneux, the nearest League ground to Ludlow, that he made his debut in the Football League on 21 February 1948. A blizzard swept over Wolverhampton before the match. Ground staff were sweeping the touch lines right up to the kick-off, and after the whistle had blown snow continued to fall and a strong wind lashed the stadium. At the final whistle the crowd totalled just over 24,000, about twice as many as at the kick-off, many having been delayed by the weather. The Wolves team included two other well-known Salopians, the right-winger Johnny Hancocks, born at Oakengates, and the England captain Billy Wright, a native of Ironbridge. Cyril played at his accustomed position, inside-left, and contributed significantly to a 4-2 victory for Everton, showing 'some nice touches' according to one reporter. A Merseyside journalist concluded that he was 'the Everton type, good ball control, a nice passer of the ball and one with a fighting quality'. A party of Cyril's friends from Ludlow travelled through the snow to watch the match. Afterwards Cyril returned to his parents' home on their coach, and Bill Badlan proudly recalls sitting next to him on the journey.

Cyril's home debut for Everton's first team was even more full of promise. At Goodison on 28 February 1948 they faced a Middlesbrough team flushed with confidence after beating Liverpool on their previous visit to Merseyside. After Middlesbrough had opened the scoring, Cyril equalised with a header and went on to score the winner. A newspaper headline ran 'New Everton Man's Bright Home Debut – Accepted His Chance...Story-book first appearance'. One reporter noted that every Everton supporter left Goodison talking about the 'young' Cyril Lello, and praised his creative ideas and his ball control. Another warned against excessive optimism about an unknown 'youngster' after just two first team games, but considered that his ball control, deft touches, dribbling and intelligent positioning augured well for his future. A third reporter concluded that his play had the hallmark of class and that Middlesbrough lost because they had no one who could match his speed, craft and shooting power, a significant compliment since their inside-left was the much-capped England player Wilf Mannion.

Cyril Lello's success in these two games established his place for a time in Everton's first team. He played in every game during March 1948, but was then dropped. On 21 April he played at centre -forward in a humiliating 0-4 home defeat against Liverpool and three days later was restored to his inside-left position in a 0-1 defeat against Portsmouth at Goodison, before missing the two remaining games of the season. Everton finished in fourteenth position in Division One, after winning only one of their last five games.

*Everton team photograph
1951-52.
Back row: left to right:
H E Cooke (trainer),
J M McIntosh, T E Jones,
H Potts, E Sagar, C F Lello,
E Moore, W M Lindley,
J A Grant; front row: left to
right:- T J Eglington, J S Lindsay,
H Catterick, J W Parker,
E Buckle, P D Farrell (captain),
A W Fielding.*

During the autumn of 1948 responsibility for Everton's first team passed from Theo Kelly to a new manager, Cliff Britton. The season had a disastrous beginning. Everton lost six of their first eight matches, scoring only five goals while conceding 25. A crowd of 57,729 were attracted to Goodison for the first game of the season, but less than 25,000 saw Everton defeated by Stoke City on 13 September. Cyril Lello first played in the third game of the season, at inside-right in an away defeat at Middlesbrough on 28 August. He reverted to inside-left to experience a resounding 0-5 home defeat by Birmingham City on 5 September. He was relegated to the reserves for much of the autumn during which the team staged a slow recovery, but appeared at centre-forward in a goalless draw with Manchester City on Christmas Day.

Cliff Britton was a skilful tactician who re-shaped the team. Cyril Lello thought highly of him, and was grateful for the way in which the manager gave a new direction to his career during the difficult season of 1948-49. In the second Merseyside Derby of the season, a goalless draw at Anfield on 5 February 1949, Cyril Lello played his first game for the first team since Christmas Day wearing a No 6 shirt, indicating that he had moved to left-half, something which had evidently been rehearsed in practice matches from which the press had been excluded. To his right was Tommy Jones, the burly Welsh centre half, while at right half was the Irishman, Peter Farrell. Everton have been proud of several half-back lines during the club's long history, notably that of Howard Kendall, Joe Harvey and Alan Ball which controlled so many matches during the late 1960s, but that of Farrell, Jones and Lello served the club as well as any. Everton concluded the season in 18th place in Division One, a creditable achievement for Cliff Britton after a distressing beginning. A month after his first game at left-half, Cyril's photograph appeared on the cover of the match programme for their game with Blackpool on 5 March 1949.

Cyril Lello aged 30.

Britton continued to play Farrell, Jones and Lello in mid-field in the season that commenced on 20 August 1949 with a 1-0 victory at Middlesbrough. Just once, Cyril reverted to his old inside-left position, for the return match, a 3-1 win at Goodison on 17 December, but then resumed his place in the half-back line. On 28 February he was kicked on the knee while trying to block a shot in a 1-1 home draw with Aston Villa, and had to leave the field in the 27th minute of the match. He missed seven League games, an FA Cup quarter-final against Tottenham Hotspur and the subsequent semi-final against Liverpool, but resumed his place at left-half in a 3-0 home win against Blackpool on 7 April, and played out the rest of the season. Everton again finished 18th in Division One, and Cyril appeared 35 times in League games and in two FA Cup ties.

The injury proved to be worse than had been anticipated. Cyril Lello underwent a cartilege operation, and then endured a long period of convalescence, during which he spent some time at a rehabilitation centre in Wolverhampton. He did not appear in Everton's first team during the whole of the 1950-51

Everton team photograph of the early 1950s - in training. Can you recognise: Cyril Lello, Peter Farrell, Ied Sagar, Tommy Eglington, Jackie Grant, Tommy Jones?

season, although he played several times in the reserves as he slowly returned to fitness. His presence was missed. Everton finished 22nd in Division One, and consequently suffered relegation.

Cyril Lello's first game in Division Two was in Everton's opening match of the season on 18 August 1951, a 0-1 defeat at Southampton, but both he and his manager realised that his return to match fitness was incomplete, and he reverted to the reserve team until the end of September, when he resumed his place in the half-back line with Peter Farrell and Tommy Jones, and played for six consecutive games, the last of which was a 1-5 home defeat against Notts County on 20 October 1951. He did not play again until Boxing Day when he took part in a 1-1 home draw against Doncaster Rovers, but missed the next two games. On 19 January 1952 he played at left-half in a 3-0 home win against Cardiff, after which one reporter commented that Cyril was now back to his best, and that Cliff Britton had been wise to allow him so much time to play himself back into the game. He retained his place for the rest of the season, in which he made a total of only 21 appearances. He played an outstanding part in a 2-0 defeat of Leicester City at Goodison on 9 February. A match against Swansea on 29 March proved a source both of pride and embarrassment. He scored the winning goal, but previously he scored an own goal, when a back-pass was lifted by a gust of wind over the goalkeeper. Everton's hope of an immediate return to the top division were frustrated, when they finished only 7th in Division Two.

At the first game of this season Cyril met up with his old schoolfriend Alf Pilson, who had left Ludlow before the war to work in the motor trade in Birmingham and subsequently in Manchester. During his military service Alf met his bride-to-be, Lily, and after demobilisation the couple made their home at Poole on the south coast. When Everton played at Southampton, on 18 August 1951,

Alf and Lily went to The Dell, and chatted with Cyril before the match, but had to leave just before the final whistle in order to catch a train home.

The 1952-53 season proved equally frustrating both for the club and for Cyril Lello, who played in the opening game, a 0-2 home defeat against Hull City, but did not appear again until he played at Plymouth and in a home draw with Leeds United in mid-November. He then missed two more games, but returned for a cheering 5-0 away win at Bury on 13 December, and retained his place for the rest of the season, usually alongside Peter Farrell and Tommy Jones. He made 26 league appearances, and at the end of the season Everton secured 16th place in Division Two.

Everton enjoyed a good run in the FA cup beating Aston Villa, Nottingham Forest and Manchester United en route to a semi-final against Bolton Wanderers. One reporter regarded Cyril Lello as the outstanding player in Everton's 4-1 defeat of Nottingham Forest in a tie on 31 January, after the team had enjoyed a spell of special pre-match training at Harrogate. Before the semi-final against Bolton Wanderers at Maine Road, Manchester on 21 March 1953 the players trained at Brighton, where they spent much of their time on the golf course, but did more serious preparation at the Hove greyhound stadium. The *Ludlow Advertiser* noted that the town was proud of Cyril and that his friends were looking forward to his winning an FA Cup medal. Players' wives, including Elsie Lello, were taken by coach from Goodison to enjoy lunch at the Queen's Hotel in Manchester prior to the game. The semi-final proved to be one of the most dramatic matches of Cyril Lello's career. At half-time, thanks largely to the energy of Nat Lofthouse, Bolton were winning by 4-0, but Everton recovered, and the final result was a 3-4 defeat. Everton, and Cyril, thus failed to make their way into the Coronation year FA Cup Final, one of the most memorable games played at Wembley, in which, at the last gasp, Bolton were beaten by Blackpool and Stanley Matthews.

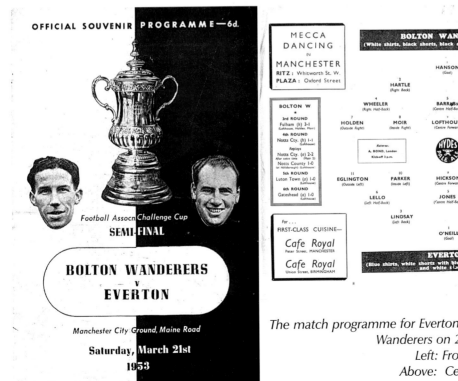

The match programme for Everton's FA Cup semi-final against Bolton Wanderers on 21 March 1953.
Left: Front cover
Above: Centre pages.

In his early years at Everton Cyril Lello shared lodgings with Tommy Clinton and Jackie Grant, but his life changed in 1950 with his marriage. His bride was Elsie Healey from Kirkdale, who had worked as a clerk for Vernons Pools. She had long been an Everton supporter, and had done part-time work at Goodison Park. The couple had met at a Supporters' Club dance. Rumours current in Ludlow for many years that Cyril had married the daughter of his manager, a coach or a director were quite false. The wedding took place at St John's Roman Catholic Church in Melrose Road, Kirkdale. Elsie's sister Millie Furlong, was matron of honour, and her brother-in-law was best man.

Elsie and Cyril Lello at an Everton social function c 1956.

Her niece, in a satin dress in Everton colours, presented her with a horseshoe. Guests included Cyril's team-mates Jackie Grant and Wally Fielding, and his brothers Harold and Les. The couple settled in a club house on the edge of the stadium at No 18 Goodison Avenue that had previously been occupied by Theo Kelly, and was rather better fitted out than other club houses. Their only child, a boy christened Cyril Francis in accordance with Roman Catholic practice, rather than Cyril Frank after his father, was born on 24 March 1954.

Cyril's life was transformed in many other respects by his move to Merseyside. In Shrewsbury the football club was well-regarded, particularly when its elevation to Football League status appeared imminent, but this was as nothing compared with the adulation accorded to members of the Liverpool and Everton clubs on Merseyside. Just occasionally, usually for a local derby against Walsall, the Gay Meadow at Shrewsbury accommodated crowds of 18,000. The attendance at Goodison for Cyril's home debut match was 43,634, and in due course he was to play there in front of crowds of over 70,000. Before cup ties Everton players were often taken to train at resorts, at Brighton, Harrogate or Buxton where Cyril was once photographed in a double-breasted suit sampling the waters with some of his colleagues. Everton and Liverpool players were invited each season to receptions at the town hall. They went to special showings of films in the city's cinemas, and were provided with ringside seats for circus performances at the Liverpool Stadium. Cyril and Elsie attended a dinner given by the Lord Mayor at the town hall on 4 May 1954 to mark Everton's promotion to the First Division. There were also social events when overseas teams visited Merseyside to play against Everton, usually in May just after the end of a season. On 12 March 1955 for example, there was a dinner at the Exchange Hotel, marking a match between Everton and the Swedish team SV Sodingen.

Left: Cyril Lello and colleagues taking the waters at Buxton while preparing for their FA Cup tie with Manchester City on 3 March 1956. Left to right:- Jimmy Harris, Jimmy Tansey, Eddie Wainwright, John Willie Parker, Cyril Lello, Gladys Jones (attendant), Jimmy O'Neill (behind attendant).

Below: Cyril Lello, posed with the fishing rod which reminded him of his boyhood at Dinham Mill (Liverpool Echo 22 October 1955).

Nevertheless before the abolition of the maximum wage in 1961, the life style of a successful professional footballer was necessarily modest. In October 1955 the *Liverpool Echo* described the life of the Lello family at No 18 Goodison Avenue, showing a picture of Cyril wearing a Fair Isle sweater and holding a fishing rod. He recalled that he had become an enthusiastic angler as a boy living by the River Teme in Ludlow, but regretted that fishing in the nearby Leeds & Liverpool Canal produced only bedsteads and old bikes. He was also sorry that his club house lacked a garden, denying to his son the opportunities for the outdoor life he had enjoyed as a boy. Nevertheless he kept a dog, a Sealyham terrier called 'Corporal'. The house, like many at the time, apparently lacked a television set. Cyril told the *Echo* reporter that he enjoyed woodwork, crosswords and reading, notably westerns. There was a piano in the house, which Elsie could play well, and the couple enjoyed going out to dances, on which occasions members of Elsie's family looked after young Cyril.

Cyril and Elsie Lello solving a crossword puzzle at their home in Goodison Avenue as depicted by the Liverpool Echo on 22 October 1955.

Cyril had travelled in Europe with the RAF Regiment, but as an Everton player he saw a succession of overseas countries in very different circumstances. He appears to have gone to Sweden with Everton in 1950. On 15 May 1954 he was one of 16 players who left Lime Street station for Euston at the start of a tour of Denmark. They stayed the night at the Waldorf Hotel in London, and saw a show at the Palace Theatre, before going to Liverpool Street station the following afternoon to take 'The Scandinavian' which delivered them to the *SS Kronprins Frederik*, on which they spent the night en route to Esbjerg. They played three games in Jutland, before taking a night steamer from Aalborg to Copenhagen, where they played a match on 30 May that was followed by a magnificent dinner at the Hotel Cosmopolite. Cyril found that the weather in the Danish capital in late May was too hot for football.

The following year 16 players left Liverpool on 6 May, for a more complex tour, following a similar route to Esbjerg, although without an overnight stay in London. They stayed in Aarhus where they played a match against the city team, and the following day went to Copenhagen. They travelled by train to Germany, where they played a match at Schweinfurt. They crossed the Austrian border to play in Salzburg, and returned to Germany for matches in Augsburg and Cologne, before ending the tour with a game against Holland Sport, while staying in Scheveningen. They sailed to Harwich on the overnight ferry on 25 May, and returned from Harwich direct to Liverpool on the 'North Country Continental'.

The tour of 1956 was even more ambitious. On 18 May the team left Lime Street for London on the 'Merseyside Express' before going to Southampton where they joined the *Queen Elizabeth*. Cyril was photographed with a group of his team mates enjoying pints in one of the bars on the *Queen Elizabeth*. Everton's tour was sponsored by the American Soccer League. They played ten matches in four American states and three Canadian provinces, four of them against Aberdeen FC, one of them on the shores of the Pacific Ocean in the Empire Stadium, Vancouver. The tour lasted for almost a month, and the team arrived back in Liverpool on 17 June.

Cyril was a talented cricketer. He made guest appearances during holidays in Ludlow with the Dolphins, a team formed in 1945, most of whose original members worked for the Shropshire, Staffordshire & Worcestershire electricity company, whose employees, together with Midland Red bus crews, were accustomed to take refreshment in Chapman's Café in Upper Galdeford, which had formerly been the Dolphin Inn. The club aimed to provide 'really good cricket at a price which the working man can afford'. Cyril's brother Leslie, who, like his father and brother Harold, worked for the electricity company, was a founder member, and served as vice-captain of the club in 1948 and as captain in 1950. Harold who was not demobilised until early 1947, kept wicket in the 1947, 1948, 1949, 1950 and 1951 seasons. Les was an accomplished bowler who took 28 wickets at 7.21 in the 1949 season, in which Harold was the most successful batsmen with an average of 20.25. Harold could also bowl when the occasion arose. In a match against Knighton in July 1947 the Dolphins' attack was fading. Harold was asked to

Les and Harold Lello ready to take the field for the Dolphins Cricket Club c 1950.

discard his pads and gloves and take a turn with the ball, which he did with effect, taking six wickets for 36. In June 1949 Cyril Lello played with his two brothers for the Dolphins against Cleobury Mortimer. The *Ludlow Advertiser* reported that the Dolphins team included Cyril Lello the Everton footballer, who 'proved to be an excellent bowler, keeping a good length and causing the batsmen to keep on the defensive'. The Ludlow team had an easy victory after dismissing their opponents for 30 runs, with Cyril taking three wickets for 12. In June 1950 he showed his capabilities with the bat when he scored 19 not out in a victory against Brampton Bryan. By repute Cyril once hit six sixes in an over in a match at Brampton Bryan off an aristocratic bowler who complained that such play was 'not cricket' but this event appears not to have been noticed in the local press. He also played cricket for Everton. An XI made up of the club's players traditionally played a two-evening match against the Bootle Cricket Club each season. Cyril was a member of the team in 1954 and 1955 and perhaps in other seasons.

The Football League seasons that began in 1953, 1954 and 1955 marked the zenith of Cyril Lello's career. When football resumed in the summer of coronation year he was already 33 years of age, an advanced age for a footballer. Merseyside newspapers had ceased to refer to him as a 'youngster'. He missed only five League games in the three seasons, and took part in 12 FA Cup ties. His opponents included some of the most celebrated players in the history of English football, and he was universally judged to be the equal of most of them. These were the years of Everton's recovery, and while the team in which Lello played won no trophies, they did restore the club's reputation as the 'school of science'. Their style of play was widely praised.

In all but six games of the 1953-54 season Cyril Lello played at left-half alongside Peter Farrell and Tommy Jones. He made an enforced change of position in one early game, against Oldham on 29 August, when, in the days before substitutes, he went to hobble on the right wing following a leg injury. His anticipation was nevertheless unimpaired, and when Tommy Eglinton after a dazzling run down the left wing rather over-hit his cross, Cyril was at hand, 'lonely as an Everton fan at Anfield' to nod the ball

Cyril Lello as he appeared in a series of colour prints of footballers in the mid-1950s published in Charlie Buchan's Football Monthly.

to the foot of John Willie Parker, who shot it into the Oldham net. Six minutes later, while still hobbling, he made the goal that completed Parker's hat-trick and gave Everton a 3-1 victory. He scored with a shot from 40 yards in a 3-2 home win against Derby County on 26 September, of which one correspondent remarked 'I never want to see a Second Division match more worthy of First Division billing'. The manner in which Cyril Lello 'joyously ploughed through mud' to secure a home draw against Bury in January 1954 was praised by the *Liverpool Echo* correspondent, who was also impressed with the way in which he subdued the threat of Ivor Allchurch in an FA Cup tie against Swansea on 30 January, keeping his feet throughout the match, and in spite of his marking duties, taking many opportunities to turn defence into attack. His move to half-back had naturally reduced the number of goals he scored, but he raised many cheers at Goodison when he contributed one of the eight goals scored against Plymouth Argyll on 27 February 1954. As the season drew to a close, it was evident that Everton would probably win promotion, although they failed to go up as champions. Several commentators noted Cyril Lello's contribution to the team's success. He was regarded as one of the factor's behind Everton's revival. Don Kendall of the *Liverpool Echo* praised his drive, and rated him as 'one of the game's strongest tacklers, with few superiors amongst English left half backs', who had enjoyed a 'grand season' which might help him to forget his long-lasting injury. One of Cyril's outstanding performances was in the last home game of the season against Birmingham City, when, in front of 63,000 people, he combined with Tommy Eglington in a move which enabled the dashing Dave Hickson to put a thunderous header past the celebrated Blues goalkeeper Gil Merrick for what proved to be the only goal of the game.

The telegram sent to Cyril Lello by Jim Laver before Everton's promotion match at Oldham on 29 April 1954.

By this time promotion was eagerly anticipated. Everton's second and third teams had already won the Central League and the West Cheshire League. The final game of the season, at Boundary Park, Oldham, on Thursday 29 April 1954, proved to be another highlight in Cyril Lello's career. In the dressing room he received a telegram from Jim Laver, president of the South Shropshire League, wishing him well on behalf of his old friends in Ludlow. The East Lancashire Road was described as 'one vast jam of coaches, cars, brakes, lorries, vans, three-wheelers, motor cycles and push bikes' as about 30,000 Evertonians, of whom about 5,000 were unable to get into the ground, made their way to Oldham, where they ate up the snack bars and drank dry the pubs. Everton, playing in white, won 4-0, and the players had to run from the field when the final whistle blew to avoid being engulfed by their deliriously happy supporters. Peter Farrell, the captain, said that it was the best moment of his life. Along the East Lancashire Road the Everton supporters 'rode triumphantly back, telling the tale of glory in every pub on the way to Liverpool, to Goodison Park and to the First Division'. The next day the entire playing staff departed on a weekend trip to London which included a visit to Wembley for the FA Cup Final, in which the winning goal for West Bromwich Albion was scored by their winger Frank Griffin, like Cyril a former Shrewsbury Town player, who remembers Cyril as a formidable opponent.

The Everton team in the dressing room at Boundary Park on 29 April 1954 after the 4-0 defeat of Oldham Athletic which secured their promotion to Division One. Cyril Lello (on the right) has already dressed.

Everton began the following season with a 5-2 away victory at Sheffield United, which according to one report showed that they were a 'genuine First Division side in every respect'. The half-back line of Farrell, Jones and Lello controlled the game, and a perceptive pass by Cyril Lello enabled John Willie Parker to score the opening goal. The first home game of the season on 28 August proved to be another of the high points of Cyril's career. A crowd of 76,969 gathered to witness the return of First Division football to Goodison. Cyril, regarded by this time as 'that yeoman half-back (and shooter)', played one of his best games for the club, and scored the only goal with a powerful 25-yard drive ten minutes from the end. Cyril Lello was judged by the press to have been one of the two best players on the field along with Tom Finney, who played at outside-right for Preston. Cyril faced other formidable opponents on the right side of the Preston team. Tommy Docherty played at right-half, while at right-back was Willy Cunningham who had captained Scotland in the World Cup in Switzerland earlier in the year. A party of Cyril's friends and relations travelled in two coaches from Ludlow to see the game. The trip like many other outings from Ludlow, was organised by Fred Heath, landlord of the Star & Garter in Corve Street. The regular drivers of the Corvedale Motors coaches used for trips from the pub were Deany Burton and Gordon Tipton, both of whom in pre-war days had played amateur football alongside Cyril Lello. Cyril chatted with several of his old friends before the game and copies of the match programme are still treasured in Ludlow.

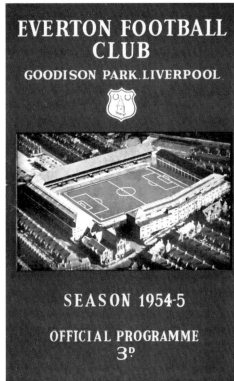

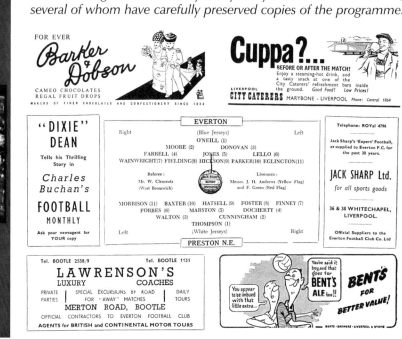

The match programme for Everton's First Division match against Preston North End on 28 August 1954. Left: Front cover. Below: Centre pages. This was the game attended by many of Cyril's friends from Ludlow, several of whom have carefully preserved copies of the programme.

The Everton half-backs dominated the game when the team gained a 2-0 victory over Chelsea at Stamford Bridge on 18 September, and when, on 16 October, Everton beat Sunderland 1-0 at Goodison, a Liverpool supporter wrote to Cyril Lello congratulating him on the way in which he had played against Len Shackleton, 'the best inside forward in the game'. On 30 October the half-backs again controlled the game when Everton gained a decisive 4-2 victory over Manchester United, whose team included Denis Viollet, who was in brilliant form, Jack Rowley, and the precociously talented Duncan Edwards, one of the victims of the Munich air crash in February 1958. On 21 November Cyril Lello, breaking up attack after attack, was mainly responsible for securing a draw against West Ham, when for the last 20 minutes of the match, his team lacked both its centre half, Tommy Jones, and its centre forward, Dave Hickson, who had both been injured. The 'mighty Everton halfback line' was reported to be 'the rock on which this tenth victory was erected' when they beat Sheffield Wednesday 3-1 on 11 December. The team secured a memorable Christmas double, beating Wolves, at home on Christmas Day and at Molyneux on 27 December. Wolves were then heading Division One, and had recently beaten the Hungarian side Honved and Spartak Moscow. The game at Goodison was judged to be one of the best that Cyril had played for Everton, his achievement in marking the talented Peter Broadbent being particularly noteworthy, while at Molyneux the 'fast and clever' Dave Hickson played so well that Billy Wright decided to man-mark him, thus affording Cyril an opportunity to score.

The most influential tactical development of the 1954-55 League season was the 'Revie plan' adopted by Manchester City, in which Don Revie, later manager of Leeds United and England, played as a deep-lying centre forward, distributing the ball to his fellow attackers. Cyril Lello judged that Cliff Britton's preparation with his team of a plan to counter the threat posed by Revie was a mark of his skill as a coach. On 23 February 1955 Everton beat Manchester City 1-0 at Goodison. It was Cyril who was given the task of neutralising Don Revie. Headlines announced 'Lello put Kybosh on Revie Plan' and 'Revie Plan Scotched; Lello Spiked the Wheels in Narrow Victory'. Cyril's photograph appeared in a Sunday newspaper, the caption describing him as 'the Everton half-back who curbed and beat the Revie Plan at Goodison Park yesterday'. Peter Farrell declared that 'Everywhere that Revie went he always found Cyril Lello close by', while the reporter George Follows commented that 'Revie was the hub of the wheel but the wheel was broken'. The *Daily Herald* reporter wrote on the following Monday that 'It was Lello who saw to it that the Revie Plan was a failure', concluding that he was 'the best uncapped left-half in England'. Perhaps no other game brought Cyril Lello so much attention. He later discussed it with his old schoolfriend, Bill Nash, to whom he modestly confided that marking Don Revie was one of the easier tasks he had been asked to undertake during his Everton career.

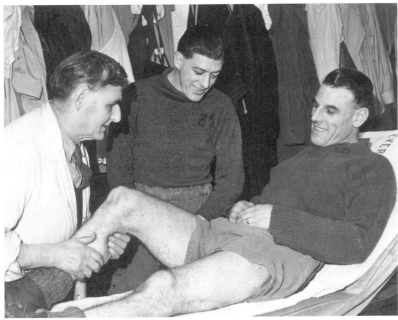

Cyril Lello on the treatment table at Everton during the 1955-56 season.

Everton were regarded as potential champions in February but their performances fell away in the final two months of the season and they finished 11th, a creditable position for a club that had just been promoted.

The following season started badly for Everton when they were beaten 0-4 by Preston North End at Goodison. They had sold Dave Hickson to Aston Villa, and their need of sharp-shooting strikers was much remarked. Their revival began on 10 September with a 2-0 win at The Valley against Charlton Athletic for whom the celebrated Sam Bartram was in goal. Commentators were full of praise for the traditional half-back line of Farrell, Jones and Lello, commending the way in which the three retained possession of the ball, contributing magnificently to defence, but with a constant urge to drive forward in attack. In two reports Cyril Lello was rated the best player on the field. The half-backs were similarly commended in subsequent matches against Portsmouth, Aston Villa and a Tottenham Hotspur team which included Danny Blanchflower and Tony Marchi in its half-back line. A reporter on the latter match described 'the driving wheel Farrell, reliable Jones, and the man who is always chipping in, little Lello'. The three imposed similar domination on the distinguished Tottenham midfield in the return match at White Hart Lane the following January. In a review of the first part of the season in November 1955 a commentator wrote of Peter Farrell and Cyril Lello that 'they play so well, week after week, that they do not always get the credit they deserve' noting that it was due largely to the half-backs that Everton had recovered from their disappointing start to the season.

It was at the Spurs match at White Hart Lane on 21 January 1956 that an incident occurred which illustrates Cyril's good nature. A 12-year-old boy from Essex had written to him for his autograph after seeing him play for Everton against Arsenal at Highbury. Cyril offered to meet him next time that Everton played in London, and waited at the gates of White Hart Lane with tickets for him and his father, but they were delayed by a coach breakdown, and the game had already begun when they arrived. Although the boy had a slight disability, which prevented him from playing football himself, Cyril had gained the impression that it was greater than it was. The incident was reported in the *Daily Mirror* and in the *Essex & Thurrock Gazette*. The following August the Essex family spent a holiday with relations at Port Sunlight. Again Cyril offered tickets for a match, this time at Goodison, and

Cyril Lello in action at Highbury.

again the family were delayed when their car broke down in the Mersey Tunnel, and were too late for the match. Elsie entertained them at No 18 Goodison Avenue, and when Cyril arrived, straight from the changing room, he perceived that the boy's father had exaggerated his disability, but was nevertheless protective to the boy himself, and took him on a tour of Goodison the following week, introducing him to all the players and collecting their autographs for him in a tiny notebook, which still survives, but Cyril himself modestly avoided signing. Cyril went on to the pitch with the boy who recalls:

I can't remember everything we talked about but the Arsenal and Tottenham games came up. He did ask me what I was going to do in the future, so I said I'm never going to make a footballer, but what I really want to be is a merchant seaman. I'm going away to sea as soon as I'm old enough. It came right from the heart. His answer was 'That's good. You do that. That's good'.

The boy did exactly that and enjoyed eight 'great and happy years' with the P & O company. 'Cyril Lello... needs to be remembered' he wrote, 44 years later, 'Who else would have gone to all that trouble for a lad, even in the belief that he was crippled?'

Cyril Lello contributed substantially to Everton's run in the FA Cup in the early months of 1956. On

No. **1010**

TOTTENHAM HOTSPUR FOOTBALL & ATHLETIC COMPANY, LTD.

Admit Bearer to

RESERVED STAND

Block F

Row R

Seat No. **23**

WEST STAND—ENTRANCE HIGH ROAD

Complimentary

VISITING CLUB

Secretary

One of the complimentary tickets provided by Cyril Lello for his young admirer from Essex for the match between Everton and Tottenham Hotspur on 21 January 1956.

7 January 1956 in a match against Bristol City that was judged to be a particularly splendid cup tie, he effectively marked the formidable John Atyeo while seeming to have twice as much of the ball as any other player, although a leg injury isolated him on the wing for the last 20 minutes. He again played well in the next round when Everton beat Port Vale 3-2 at Vale Park. The next cup tie, in which a 1-0 victory was secured against Chelsea at Goodison, was his 150th consecutive game for Everton's first team. Cliff Britton paid tribute to Cyril's devotion to the club, and concluded that he was still jumping higher and covering more ground than ever and that he had never seen the wing-half play better. This match took place on the eve of Britton's resignation. The club were planning the tour which took Cyril and his colleagues across America, and the directors proposed to bring in a temporary manager to attend to affairs at Goodison while the tourists were away. In February Cliff Britton took exception to the proposal and resigned, to be replaced by Ian Buchan.

Cyril played five more games before his run of 155 consecutive appearances came to an end in mid-March after an injury in training. Only Neville Southall, Everton's goalkeeper in the 1980s exceeded this total, with 212 consecutive games for the first team. Third in the list of consecutive appearances is the striker, Joe Royle. With the growth of the squad system it is doubtful whether any outfield player will exceed Cyril's total. Cyril Lello played 254 Football League and FA Cup games for Everton, but this total has been passed by many other players, some of whom began their careers with the club.

Cyril soon returned to the first team, but missed the last four games of the season. Peter Farrell switched to play at left-half while K Birch replaced him at right-half. On 28 April he showed that his shooting powers were undiminished when, after six years as a half-back, he played at inside-left and scored a hat-trick at Goodison in a friendly match against the Brazilian team Vasco da Gama, which Everton won 6-3. Everton did well after their bad start to finish the season in 15th position in the First Division.

Everton team photograph 1956.

Cyril Lello was now 36 years of age. He had enjoyed a remarkable run of consecutive games in the first team, but was increasingly prone to injury. Neither he nor Everton enjoyed the opening of the 1956-57 season, but while the club survived, his own career in the First Division came to an end. For the first game, at Leeds United, the familiar half-back line of Farrell, Jones and Lello appeared on the team sheet but Everton were beaten 1-5. Ian Buchan directed the team coach to stop about two miles from Elland Road, and ordered the players to walk the remaining distance to the ground. Cyril played in the next three games, two of which were lost and one drawn, but he missed the next two, both defeats. On 8 September he played in his old position of inside-left in a 0-4 home defeat by Aston Villa, which proved to be his last game for the first team. Everton recovered from another disastrous start and finished the season in the same position as in 1955-56. In most matches from 20 October when they beat Manchester United 5-2, the half-back line comprised K Birch, Tommy Jones and Peter Farrell. Cyril left Everton early in November 1956 to join Rochdale, who were managed by Harry Catterick, the centre-forward for whom nine years previously he had made two goals in his debut match in the Central League at Molyneux.

Just after Cyril Lello left Everton for Rochdale his former captain Peter Farrell described his memorable and uncomplaining service to Everton, rating him as 'one of the finest club men ever to wear a blue jersey'. On the field he was hard in the tackle, but 'never guilty of a shady action', while he never entered into disputes with training staff or club officials. Sam Rogers who came from Hanwood near Shrewsbury, was a Football League referee in the 1950s. He had charge of several First Division games involving Everton, and recalls that while Cyril Lello was fully committed to gaining victory for his team, he never did anything that demanded a reprimand from the referee. Cyril's nature off the field was easy-going, and he was generally known on Merseyside as 'Lol'. He had a dry sense of humour – his schoolfriend Bill Nash recalls that once when he was pressured to say what he would like to be when he grew up he replied 'a retired bank manager'. There was general agreement that this undemonstrative wing-half contributed much to Everton's revival. Commentators agreed about his footballing qualities, his sure-footedness, his hard and effective tackling, his ability to pass accurately, his powerful throw-in, his uncanny ability to be in the right position, his stamina which enabled him to play as energetically in the ninetieth minute of a match as in the first, and the powerful shooting perfected when he was a striker and in his boyhood against the wall of Dinham Mill. He also contributed what modern football tacticians would call a high work rate. He enjoyed playing at wing-half because it meant that he was always involved in the play, whether in defence or in attack. He felt that one of the strengths of his game was his ability to keep close up behind his forwards and to feed passes to them. His versatility was remarkable. His school friend Jack Reynolds said that he could play anywhere. Cyril was proud that he had been a centre-half in schoolboy and youth teams, and he was to return to that position at Runcorn. He played in every forward position for Shrewsbury. He was an inside-left when he went to Everton, and became a left-half, but also started games at left-back, right-half, inside-right and centre-forward. He once stood in as an emergency goalkeeper for Everton, and was to do so again for Rochdale. On several occasions he made useful contributions to matches when hobbling on the wing after being injured. He enjoyed playing against the celebrated players of his time, even against Stanley Matthews, although he admitted that 'you just couldn't win them all with him'. He was amused by the antics of Len Shackleton, remembering that he once confused an Everton defender by pretending to look at a watch on his wrist. In the days when wing-halves traditionally marked inside-forwards, he regarded Ivor Broadis and George Robledo as two of the opponents he most admired.

Many competent judges considered that Cyril Lello should have been given international recognition. His League debut match at Molyneux was watched by the secretary of the Welsh FA who reputedly expressed disappointment when he found that he came from Ludlow on the English side of the border. In 1948 when England were due to play the Irish Republic at Goodison one Merseyside journalist considered that he had an excellent chance of a cap, and throughout 1953 and 1954 reporters who saw him play considered that he would distinguish himself at international level. In 1955 and 1956 their tone changed a little and they began to express their puzzlement that he had missed representative honours. Age was probably a significant factor. Cyril was 28 when he made his debut in the First Division. He was four years older than his fellow-Salopian Billy Wright, who won his first cap when he was 22, in the first peacetime international in September 1946, long before Cyril enjoyed a regular place in a First Division team. In the early 1950s, when Billy Wright normally played at centre-half for England, the left-half position was usually occupied by Jimmy Dickinson, a member of the successful Portsmouth team of the time, who was five years younger than Cyril, and first represented his country in May 1949. During Cyril's last season of First Division football the England half-back line was adorned by the talents of the young Duncan Edwards, no less than 16 years his junior. While Cyril's spell in the RAF in some ways helped his development as a professional footballer, in other respects his war service was an interruption to a career that already in 1939 was progressing well, and had he been playing for a First Division team rather earlier he might have gained England honours. Nevertheless during his three best seasons for Everton he played against Stanley Matthews, Tom Finney, Nat Lofthouse, Len Shackleton, Tommy Docherty, Dave Sexton, Denis Viollet, Duncan Edwards, Danny Blanchflower and many others whose names are still well known. He was respected in such company.

6. A Veteran Footballer

Cyril Lello moved to Rochdale at a time of great expectations. The town was preparing to celebrate the centenary of its charter during 1957, while the football club was anticipating its 50th anniversary. On Friday 9 November 1956 Rochdale was alive with rumours since Harry Catterick was 'away on business'. It was anticipated that he was going to sign the ex-Everton centre forward John Willie Parker, then with Bury, but in the event he brought Cyril Lello to the club, and included him in the team as left half in a 2-2 draw with Stockport County on the following day. Catterick took care to explain to the press that Cyril Lello would continue to live in Liverpool, and to do some of his training with Everton. It was a time of innovation for the football club – Cyril's debut match was the first League game at Spotland to be illuminated by floodlights. On that very day Rochdale's most celebrated daughter, Gracie Fields, concluded a centenary week of variety performances at the Hippodrome. During her stay in her home town she found time to open new premises for the town's best-known institution, the Rochdale Equitable Pioneers co-operative society. The Monday after Cyril's debut match there were disturbances at the Empire Theatre at the first showing of the Bill Haley film 'Rock Around the Clock' when 'a screaming mob of long-haired drain-piped crepe-soled dervishes', danced in the aisles and threw fireworks. Rochdale remained an important centre of textile manufacture – the monthly yarn production counts featured prominently in the local press, and there was so little unemployment that local firms offered jobs to refugees from the Russian invasion of Hungary.

Cyril Lello's first appearance cheered the optimists amongst Rochdale supporters. He played at inside-left, made one goal and had a fierce shot stopped on the line. The *Rochdale Observer* commented that 'the most recent Everton export was obviously a player of poise and purpose, intent on using the ball carefully every time he got it', and forecast that the forward line would perform some skilled work once Lello settled into the side. In the next two games Cyril demonstrated his versatility rather than his skills as a striker. In the match with Accrington Stanley on 17 November Rochdale's goalkeeper was injured in the opening minutes, conceded a goal and was then seen to be wandering, concussed, about the penalty area. Cyril took over and performed well, letting in only one further goal in the 85th minute. This match was watched by his schoolfriend Jack Reynolds, who had made his home at nearby Shaw. The following Saturday in an away match against Chester, after another injury, he played for 80 minutes at left-back and set a high standard with an exhibition of 'cultured full-back play', which brought Rochdale a 2-2 draw. Following a head injury he played at left-half for the reserves on 15 November, only four days after the removal of the stiches. He played in most of his subsequent games for the first team in that position, but the club ran into a bad spell, suffering successive away and home defeats to Wrexham on Christmas Day and Boxing Day. On 5 January he and his old friend Jackie Grant, playing at right-half, controlled the midfield at an away fixture at Gateshead, but Rochdale still suffered a 1-2 defeat. Early in February in games with Scunthorpe and Crewe he played at inside-left, but was criticised for his 'lack of zip', and in comparison with Jackie Grant he was adjudged not to have settled well into the style of football current in the Northern Section of the Third Division. By contrast, his performances for the second team were commended, and it was with Rochdale Reserves on 26 January that he made what was probably his last appearance as a player at Goodison Park, which he marked, appropriately, by scoring a goal.

There were rumours in late February that Cyril Lello would be transferred to Southport, who hoped that he might become their player-coach. He made only eleven appearances for Rochdale's first team, and in the closing weeks of the season played few games for the reserves. The club finished 13th in the Northern Section, which disappointed both directors and supporters, and the press concluded that Harry Catterick's hope of making Cyril Lello the pivot of a successful team had been frustrated. Catterick hoped to keep Cyril at Rochdale, and included him on the club's retained list in May, but Cyril was dissatisfied with the terms offered, and during the summer agreed to join the Cheshire League club, Runcorn, as player-manager.

Cyril Lello conducted his first training session at the Canal Street ground of Runcorn FC on Tuesday 30 July 1957. He seems to have been warmly welcomed at the club. He had learned to drive in the RAF, but while living in Goodison Avenue and playing for Everton had no need of a car. His new club helped him to acquire a green Standard 8, SKD 760, in which he travelled to and from his new ground using the old transporter bridge, alongside which the new steel arch, which was to transform Runcorn, was steadily taking shape. The club – known as the Linnets – had been founded in 1918, and was originally part of the recreational activities of a substantial leather-processing company, Highfield and Camden Tanneries, which at that time still owned the ground. A lottery organised by the Supporters Club contributed substantially to running costs, enabling the club to pay its way. Runcorn FC had a smart business card on which were printed the addresses and telephone numbers of the chairman and secretary, and the name of the player-manager, C F Lello. When he gave copies to friends he customarily wrote on his telephone number, Aintree 7345. From the start of the 1957-58 season the club arranged for a band to play before home matches and during half-time intervals. Attendances at Canal Street, particularly for local derby matches, were often well in excess of two thousand. The directors brought in several new players, including Tommy Clinton,

The business card of Runcorn AFC during the time that Cyril Lello was player-manager.

Cyril's one-time Everton team mate and his neighbour in Goodison Avenue, Eric Binns a centre-half who had previously played for Blackburn Rovers, and the former Wolves half-back Jimmy Dunn. The *Runcorn Weekly News* in reporting on a trial match commented that it was a long time since 'such a fabulous collection of soccer talent' had graced Canal Street, and looked forward to a good season.

Cyril made favourable first impressions on Runcorn's footballing public, both on and off the field. He was described as 'a thick-set man of purpose and few words' with a dynamic personality, and as 'a leader who can rub shoulders with the best of players'. He was praised for his positioning and the accuracy of his passing. From his first weeks at Runcorn he paid much attention to the assessment and recruitment of amateurs, perhaps harking back to his experiences in Ludlow in 1938-39 when he himself crossed the frontier between recreational and professional football.

Tommy Clinton recalls that 'We didn't pull any trees up that season'. Runcorn's performances were erratic. They suffered some heavy defeats – losing 1-7 in an away fixture with Chester Reserves for example on 28 September, and suffering a frustrating FA Cup tie against Prescot Cables on 21

September which they lost 0-1 after having possession of the ball throughout most of the game. Cyril's own performances were widely applauded. A group calling themselves 'the Boys behind the Goal' wrote to the local press after Runcorn's defeat in the Cup thanking Cyril Lello for 'your tremendous fighting spirit, coupled with intelligent classy football' which was 'an inspiration and an example to any team'. There were also some notably good performances, a 6-2 victory over Stockport County Reserves on 5 November, and a 3-1 win against Hyde, then leaders of the Cheshire League, on 1 February, about which a reporter remarked that Cyril Lello was a steadying hand in the first half but 'the clever, constructive complete wing-half after the interval'. The club enjoyed an 11-match unbeaten run at the end of the season, and there was something of a carnival atmosphere when the team defeated Winsford 3-0 in front of 2,243 spectators on Easter Monday.

During his spell at Runcorn Cyril Lello met up with many former colleagues and opponents from his days with Everton in the Football League. His team for a time included his Everton colleagues Jackie Grant and Tommy Clinton. His Welsh companion in the Everton half-back line, Tommy Jones, was for a time manager of Bangor City. The skilful Eddie Quigley managed Mossley, while Johnny Hancocks, once a dazzling winger with Wolverhampton Wanderers, played for Oswestry Town.

Cyril Lello's admirers at Runcorn considered that the greatest achievement of his four years at the club was the establishment of a reserve side and of close links with local amateur football. He inaugurated a series of summer training sessions for footballers aged between 15 and 18 on Tuesday 13 May 1958, when 35 ambitious young men came to receive his tuition at Canal Street. Ten months later he pronounced himself well-pleased with the former reserves who were establishing themselves in Runcorn's first team. The team's form during the 1958-59 season was again erratic. They were knocked out of the FA Cup by Flint Town before the end of September, and finished their Cheshire League programme in the middle of the table. At the start of the season Cyril convinced one commentator that he was 'still a good hinge on which to hang a team', and while it was remarked that in some games he seemed out of touch, he continued to give some impressive displays, notably in a match against Winsford when he 'remained so cool and gave a first class demonstration of stylish football'. Some supporters criticised the club's directors for interfering in selection matters, and Cyril Lello affirmed to the press in August 1959 that whatever may have occurred in the past, he was in full control of team affairs.

Cyril Lello in his role as player-manager of Runcorn FC.

Runcorn FC enjoyed a rather better season in 1959-60, finishing 4th in the Cheshire League, in spite of a succession of defeats during March 1960. Cyril Lello's own play continued to win commendations. The *Runcorn Weekly News* remarked after a 3-1 away win against Northwich Victoria in November that while 'a player-manager is seldom praised and often criticised', he had every reason to be satisfied with his performance. He appeared in this game at centre-half, since the usual defender Bill Hodder was injured, but in the early months of 1960 increasingly tended to play in that position. In a 3-2 away victory against Stafford Rangers in late January he was applauded for 'a centre-half display second to none, superb with the first-time clearance, uncanny with the interception'. The Supporters' Club wrote to him in December congratulating him on the team's success. He was much praised in January and in February both for his own performances and for his astute signings, at a time when headlines proclaimed 'Lightning Linnets too hot to handle', and that a 6-2 win against Wrexham Reserves could have been a cricket score. Cyril's picture in a green-and-white striped Runcorn shirt appeared in the *Runcorn Weekly News*, with a caption praising the player-manager 'whose leadership has done so much to take Runcorn up the league table'.

At the beginning of the new season in August 1960 Cyril Lello announced that he would be spending more time coaching the younger players, but that he would certainly not cease playing. Nevertheless he did not make his first appearance until late September when, 'as cool and impeccable as ever', he helped as left-back in a 2-0 defeat of Tranmere Rovers Reserves in the Cheshire League Cup. His powers of leadership on the field continued to impress. When Runcorn secured a 4-1 victory away at Buxton he urged on the players when they were leading 3-1 as if they faced defeat. Nevertheless his still-accurate passes were sometimes unappreciated by team mates less skilful than his one-time Everton colleagues. His prompting of his forwards in a 2-1 win against Oswestry in November met with few responses. Runcorn again finished the season close to the top of the table, but there was evidently dissension within the upper reaches of the club. It appears that Cyril was offered the position of player-coach, which he refused, and early in April it was announced that he would fulfil his contract with Runcorn which was due to terminate on 30 June, but would be taking up an offer of a position with a club nearer to his home in Liverpool.

Whatever disagreements there may have been within the board, or between individual directors and player-manager, Cyril left Runcorn FC in good spirits. The Supporters Club presented him with a transistor radio, recognising his four seasons of achievement. The *Runcorn Weekly News* published a picture of him, wearing a blazer with an RAF badge on the pocket, making his speech of thanks to the supporters. He made his final appearance as a player at Canal Street on 29 April when Runcorn enjoyed a 5-2 victory over Winsford. Towards the end he created some amusement by making exaggerated efforts to score a goal. After the final whistle he was clapped from the field, and the crowd sang 'For he's a Jolly Good Fellow'. Somewhat ironically, three weeks after his contract expired, the new bridge linking Runcorn with Widnes was opened, and if he had stayed with the club for another season he would have been spared the long waits to cross the Mersey on the transporter bridge, that was soon afterwards demolished.

The club that offered a position to Cyril Lello in the spring of 1961 was New Brighton FC, whose ground was situated less than four miles from his home in Goodison Avenue, but on the other side of the Mersey. New Brighton had finished bottom of the Northern Section of Division Three in the 1950-51 season. The club's application for re-election was turned down, and they were replaced by Workington. Cyril Lello joined New Brighton as player-coach and captain, but played only a handful of games for his new club. He appeared as left-half in a 3-0 away victory against Prescot Cables, in which he scored one of the goals, but in a match against Winsford United, which the team ultimately lost 0-5, he experienced severe back pain after about five minutes and had to leave the field. This was no fleeting injury but a slipped disc which made playing football impossible and brought his career to an abrupt conclusion. It was the end of his five-year career as a veteran footballer, and some 23 years had passed since his first contacts with the professional game at Hereford United and Shrewsbury Town.

Cyril Lello with his last football club, New Brighton FC, at the start of the 1961-62 season

7. A footballer in retirement

When Cyril Lello left Runcorn in 1961 to take on the lesser post of part-time player-coach at New Brighton he was 41 and doubtless sensed that he would soon have to make his living outside football. His injury at New Brighton terminated his career in the game rather more quickly than he had anticipated but he had already secured another job, as a storeman with Lee Beesley, electrical contractors who had moved to Merseyside from Coventry. The company established its headquarters in Penny Lane, a thoroughfare that was shortly to be musically immortalised. While Cyril was playing for Everton he would, like other First Division footballers, have been well-paid, in the context of working-class employment, but he would have had no opportunities to lay aside substantial sums to sustain his family when he left the game. In 1958, two years after he ceased to play at Goodison the maximum wage was raised to £20 per week during the season and £17 in the summer months. This would have been a comfortable wage for a docker or a shipbuilder, but it was a meagre reward for a career that for most men ended before the age of 40. It was not until 1961, the year when Cyril gave up the game completely, that the maximum wage was ended. The chairman of Fulham FC immediately increased to £100 the weekly wage of Johnny Haynes, then perhaps the best footballer in Division One, and the era when great riches could be made by playing football had begun.

There were few glittering opportunities for Cyril and his contemporaries when they ceased to play football. A few succeeded in football management, most notably Cyril's one-time team-mate Harry Catterick, who was in charge at Goodison Park from 1961 until 1973, and managed the magnificent teams that won the League championship in 1962-63 and 1969-70. Cyril's drive and determination made him a reasonably successful player-manager at Runcorn, but while he had the ability to lead on the field, most of those who knew him agreed that he lacked the force of personality which would have made him an effective coach, tactician or trader in players, and he encountered difficulties in dealing with some of the directors at Runcorn. Several of his contemporaries in the Everton team of the mid-1950s became landlords of pubs, and apparently at the time when he ceased playing Cyril was offered the opportunity to take on a pub, but he declined. He had never been a serious drinker and the prospect did not appeal to him. While some of his contemporaries found difficulty in making a living, Cyril quietly followed his employment at Lee Beesley, in due course moving from his job in the stores to the post of timekeeping clerk, and remained there until he retired at the age of 65 in 1985.

Cyril Lello in later years, at home in Goodison Avenue, admiring a momento of his playing days at Everton.

The end of the maximum wage in 1961 brought one indirect benefit for Cyril and his family. Everton players were no longer likely to be content with houses of modest size adjacent to Goodison Park. The focus of their activities, particularly after Harry Catterick was appointed manager, came to be at Bellefield, the club's training ground, and they visited Goodison only on match days. They were now paid at levels which enabled them to live in country houses standing in several acres. In consequence Everton FC had little use for the accommodation it owned in Goodison Avenue, and the Lello family continued to live at No 18. Cyril's wife, Elsie, died in 1969, after which his mother-in-law helped Cyril bring up his son, also Cyril, then in his mid-teens. Cyril the younger married in 1976, and continued to live at home, his two sons being born in 1979 and 1982. While Cyril maintained his connections with his family and friends, he had no wish to return to live in Ludlow, although he took little advantage of the exciting social life of Merseyside in the 1960s.

For a time Cyril coached a youth team based at his family's parish church, St Francis de Sales. A team from the school linked with the church had won the *Liverpool Echo* cup, and the parish priest, Father Matthew Loughrane, wanted to keep the boys together as a youth team and sought Cyril's assistance.

Cyril kept up his links with Everton, attending almost all of the club's home matches, which took place on his doorstep. He enjoyed the successes of Harry Catterick's elegant teams of the 1960s and early 1970s. In 1984-85 the team managed by Howard Kendall, which included Peter Reid and Neville Southall, were Division One champions, winners of the European Cup-Winners Cup, and runners-up to Manchester United in the FA Cup. As the team were about to embark on their triumphal tour of Liverpool on an open-topped bus, their captain, Kevin Ratcliffe, was photographed showing their trophies to Cyril's son and grandson. Cyril himself modestly excused himself from the photograph, just as he had from many other photographs from his schooldays onwards.

Everton captain, Kevin Ratcliffe, shows the season's trophies to Cyril Lello's son and grandson in Goodison Avenue, May 1985.

Cyril kept up links with his family in Ludlow. His father had died at the age of 71 in 1959 and soon afterwards his mother and his sister Nellie left Castle Mill Cottage for a house at Steventon. The town swimming pool was opened on the mill premises in 1961. Nellie died in 1967, but her mother remained at Steventon until her death at the age of 91 in 1977. Cyril and his family regularly spent part of their annual holidays with his parents, first at Dinham Mill and later at Steventon.

Cyril Lello was regarded with awe in Ludlow, and it is some measure of the interest taken by the townspeople in his career that so many false rumours circulated about his life in Liverpool. He was a hero to young footballers even while he was in the RAF. At that time he had played professionally only for Shrewsbury Town and Hereford United, but it is probable that his achievements with Lincoln City, particularly the news of his seven goals against Notts County in December 1943, had reached the town of his birth. John Carter who was a schoolboy during World War II and lived near Dinham Mill recalls Cyril's spells of leave from the RAF in Ludlow. 'We used to follow him everywhere' he said, 'he was like a pied piper. He was a kind gentle giant to us kids. He talked football and kicked a ball about with us'. Townspeople were even more interested in him when he was playing for Everton. His son remembers that when his father took him round the town when he was a small boy, Cyril could hardly walk ten yards without someone coming up to greet him, Ernie Page remembers waiting for the school bus to Clee Hill in Upper Galdeford, when two men passed by. His school friend nudged him and said 'That's Cyril Lello'. He recalls that 'It was like seeing royalty'. While he was in Ludlow Cyril sometimes played cricket for the Dolphins, and would meet up with some of his schoolfriends, like Bill Nash, for serious conversations about football. If his annual holiday in Ludlow happened to be during the football season, Cyril would usually take the opportunity to go to the Gay Meadow to watch a Shrewsbury Town home match.

Ludlovians also invited him to sports presentations. He sometimes presented the prizes at the final of the Pitt & Minton Cup, a football competition for local teams, that had been founded to commemorate Dennis Pitt and Gordon Minton, two Ludlovians killed during the Korean War in 1951. In August 1968 Cyril attended a darts competition and raffle arranged to raise funds for the Cosy Corner, an old people's club organised for many years by Mr E G Kershaw, Ludlow's one-time police superintendent. A photograph in the *Ludlow Advertiser* shows him at the awards ceremony, a little heavier than when he was a player, but with a full head of hair, and dressed in a smart, light-coloured, single-breasted suit.

Cyril's contributions to Everton FC were regularly recognised. The club had given him two benefits, and he was remembered in features in match programmes in 1970 and 1997. His achievements were also acknowledged from time to time at functions at the supporters' social club.

Cyril Lello, second from the right, at a presentation of darts awards in Ludlow in August 1968.
Copyright to photo reproduced by permission of 'The Ludlow Advertiser'.

In 1995 he attended a reunion at Goodison Park which brought together players who had represented Everton in the 1940s. The event was recorded in a team-style photograph taken in the club's trophy room, which shows him sitting next to Dave Hickson in the front row. The photograph also includes Jackie Grant and Tommy Clinton, with whom he once shared lodgings, his former colleagues Gordon Dugdale, Norman Greenhalgh, Ted Sagar, Alex Stevenson and Gordon Watson, and one of the most renowned of Everton players, Joe Mercer, England left-half and captain, and manager of the memorable Manchester City team of the mid-1960s, who left the club the season before Cyril arrived. Subsequently Gordon Dugdale, who was Everton's left-back when Cyril joined the club, and played in that position until mid-way through the 1949-50 season, wrote to him: *Cyril Lello, when you first took Peter Farrell's place as left-half for Everton, you also relieved me of quite a burden. Many thanks old friend! And you finished as one of the best wing-halves ever to play football'.*

A reunion of Everton veterans of the 1940s at Goodison in 1995. Back row: left to right:- Unknown, Joe Mercer, Tommy Clinton, Ted Sagar, Norman Greenhalgh, Gordon Watson, a relation of Gordon Dugdale; front row: left to right: - Jackie Grant, Alex Stevenson, Dave Hickson, Cyril Lello, Gordon Dugdale.

Shortly afterwards Cyril was suddenly taken ill, and had to leave Goodison Avenue so that he could receive constant medical care. In 1996, as the club began to extend the Goodison Park stadium, plans were announced to demolish Goodison Avenue. His family had to leave the house which had been the home of the Lellos for more than 40 years, to live in the Liverpool suburbs. An Evertonian to the end, Cyril continued to go to most home matches at Goodison Park, latterly in a wheelchair, until the end of the 1996-97 season. Cyril died in hospital on 16 August 1997. After a funeral at the church of St Francis de Sales where he had coached a boys' football team, he was buried in Everton Cemetery. He was commemorated in the programme for Everton's first home fixture of the 1997-98 season, an evening match with Manchester United on Wednesday 27 August.

8. Reflections

Most biographies of footballers are written when they are in their prime or just past it, when their judgements on colleagues and opponents and their opinions on music, fashion or other contemporary matters of concern are eagerly sought. Much writing about football focusses on the great stars of the game. This biography of Cyril Lello, written some 40 years after he gave up the professional game, and four years after his death, may therefore seem unusual. While Cyril is remembered with affection and respect by those who knew him, or were aware of his reputation in the 1940s and 50s, his name is unfamiliar to most modern followers of football, except for some who support Everton or live in Shropshire. He was not an obvious star of the game. His bustling yet creative work in midfield was rarely as memorable as the dazzling runs of Stanley Matthews, or the in-flight headers of Tommy Lawton or Dave Hickson. Yet it is evident from the opinions of his team mates and from contemporary reports on matches in which he played that he was much more than just a competent member of a top-rate team, and that his accomplished ball skills were combined with an acute positional sense and an ability to read a game shrewdly. It is not possible at this distance in time to make more precise judgements. Cyril had a droll sense of humour and would probably have been amused or puzzled that anyone should think his career worthy of commemoration.

Cyril Lello's character as a footballer was shaped by his background. While his family was certainly not wealthy, in some senses he had a privileged upbringing, in a cottage alongside running water, close to woodland and to open spaces which offered freedoms, not least the freedom to play football. He attended a school whose facilities had been enhanced by a relatively enlightened education authority, and where sport received some encouragement. In other respects he was less fortunate. Cyril Lello grew up in a world that lacked ambition. Ludlow society in the 1930s must have appeared very settled, and those who wished to register achievements in life beyond those acknowledged in that society had to leave the town, as did several of his contemporaries. The town was certainly not an acknowledged nursery of footballing talent, and its clubs had no established links to the professional game. Cyril Lello's successful career was shaped by his own ambition to play football at the highest level, and by his ability to make into opportunities circumstances that others might have regarded as misfortunes.

Cyril Lello's background dictated that he was an artisan rather than an artist, 'one of those quiet ultra-effective workers without show' as a Liverpool newspaper described him when Everton were promoted from Division Two. When he was one of the outstanding players in a match at Villa Park in March 1956 a correspondent concluded that 'Lello is one of the game's great workmen'. Cyril considered it a privilege to be able to play as a professional the game that he had loved from childhood. Arthur Hughes, did not regard himself as fortunate when encountering Cyril Lello as an opponent in amateur football in the 1930s, but appreciated his company at Shrewsbury Town in 1946-47. He recalls that Cyril did not like attention but considered that it was his duty to do a good job, to make a telling pass or a clean tackle, just as his schoolboy contemporaries might take pride in fitting a door with precision, completing a neat piece of bathroom pipework, tuning a car to perfection or setting up an elegant page of print.

Cyril never wished to return to live in Ludlow. He nevertheless had great affection for the town, evidenced by his regular holidays, and by his liking for talking about Shropshire or Shropshire people whenever the opportunity arose. Don Everall, who was 12 years younger than Cyril, had a trial spell as an amateur with Everton in September 1949, and was sitting in a café with other triallists when Cyril Lello approached and asked if he was the young man from Shrewsbury. The two swapped reminiscences of the town, and Don was flattered that a senior player should have taken notice of a mere lad. Sam Rogers recalls that when he refereed an Everton match in the 1950s at the conclusion he and Cyril would usually share a gentlemanly chat about Shropshire. In old age Cyril remembered his home town with affection. Rachel Badlan and her father are both Ludlovians and Everton season ticket holders. Before one match in 1996 Rachel, then aged ten, was taken to meet Cyril Lello in his wheelchair at the Park end at Goodison. She remembers a contented old man who asked her how Ludlow was changing, how Ludlow Town FC were progressing, and recalled matches in which he played for the Dolphins Cricket Club when Rachel's grandfather Bill Badlan was captain.

Bill Badlan, a leading light in the Dolphins Cricket Club in the post-war period, who recalls that Cyril Lello sat next to him on the supporters' coach returning to Ludlow after the Wolves v Everton game on 21 February 1948, with his granddaughter Rachel Badlan, who talked with Cyril Lello at Goodison in 1996.

Cyril Lello's life merits examination for the light it throws on a particular stage of the development of football, and for the way in which it fits into the social history of the twentieth century. It shows something of what it was like in the first half of the twentieth century to grow up, endowed with a mighty talent of whatever kind, in a relative backwater like Ludlow. It illustrates the importance of the pyramid of amateur and semi-professional football clubs that, at a time when academies and schools of excellence were unknown, provided stepping stones to the highest levels for the gifted player. Cyril's career also provides evidence of how the lives of those born in the years immediately following the Great War of 1914-18 were shaped by Hitler's war. Whether Cyril's wartime experiences helped or hindered his progress towards the highest levels of football must remain uncertain. It is clear that the RAF enabled him to attain an exceptionally high level of fitness and provided him with opportunities to play with other talented footballers, as well as taking him to places which he would never have expected to visit. It is possible that if war had not broken out his talents would have been recognised by a League club while he was playing for Shrewsbury Town, and that he might have begun to play in the Football League in his early 20s, rather than at the age of 28, but this can only be a matter for speculation.

Cyril Lello's spell at Everton earned him enduring respect at the club. He spent nine years at Goodison Park and contributed memorably to Everton's best performances between 1947 and 1956, although that was not the most glorious period in the club's history. He was one of Everton's best players in the 1953-54 season when they gained promotion from the Second Division, and in the two seasons in the First Division that followed. One of the disappointments of his career must have been that he was never on the winning side in a Merseyside Derby, but he only played in five, three defeats and two goalless draws, largely because there were no derby matches during the three seasons Everton spent in the Second Division, and they returned to the First Division at the same time that Liverpool were relegated. Everton won no formal honours during Cyril Lello's spell at the club, and his collection of medals and trophies at the end of a long career in professional football was remarkably sparse. The only medal he gained at Everton, apart from commemorative tokens for appearances in friendly matches abroad, appears to have been for his role as reserve in a representative feature for the Central League at Molyneux in 1952. It is perhaps for this reason that he treasured the trophies of his teenage years, commemorating his teams' victories in the Ludlow Thursday Charity Football Cup and the Bucknell Nurse Cup.

Even in the era of the maximum wage First Division football could still be glamorous. Footballers have always been idolised on Merseyside, and Cyril's name was in the national newspapers on most Sunday and Monday mornings for the greater part of nine years. He regularly played before crowds of more than 70,000 people. He came to experience good hotels, high standards of travel, smart golf courses, formal civic dinners and the luxuries of a transatlantic liner. He travelled with Everton to some of the most elegant cities of northern Europe, and played for the club on the shores of the Pacific Ocean in Vancouver. Footballers of his generation had no opportunities to accumulate funds that would enable them to enjoy glamourous life styles when they ceased playing. For some this presented difficulties of adjustment, but Cyril Lello, after his substantial contribution to the prosperity of Runcorn AFC, settled into an unremarkable working class job in Liverpool, and was happy to continue to live in the 'tied cottage' at Goodison, from which a few steps took him into the stadium where he could watch the home games of the club he loved, whose motto, Nil satis, nisi optimum (Only the best is good enough) epitomised his own approach to football. Everton enjoyed some good times in the 1960s, 70s and 80s, which gave him great satisfaction.

Football is about tribal identities – all over the world between August and May the Internet is consulted on Saturday evenings or Sunday mornings by Englishmen and women eager to know the results achieved by Everton, Arsenal or Manchester United, and also by those seeking news of Scunthorpe and Shrewsbury Town, of Rochdale or Runcorn. People's evenings in Seattle or their Sunday mornings in Auckland are shaped by the elation or disappointment brought by the news from England. Cyril Lello's career helps to explain the strength of such feelings. It shows that football in the 1930s had deep roots in many communities, that even in the remote Borderland, clubs were involved in some of the principal events in Ludlow's social calendar, and in raising money which sustained the meagre public health service of that time. The esteem bordering on veneration in which Cyril Lello was held in his native town shows the strength of the loyalties which can be engendered by the game.

Cyril Lello is remembered with respect by former colleagues, by opponents, and by those who saw him play, at all periods of his career. His schoolfriend Alf Pilson recalled in February 2001: 'Cyril as a footballer was unique. He could read games and moves in the game ages before any of his team and was always prepared. His balance, speed of thought and positional play were always exceptional. The only thing that stopped him getting a schoolboy international cap was because he was not in a city or large town. He was in the outback'. Cyril's modesty and affability, as well as his exceptional footballing talents are recalled by Ted Daines and Joe Morris who knew him in the RAF and by Arthur Hughes, his companion during his short full-time spell with Shrewsbury Town. His Everton team mates Dave Hickson and Tommy Clinton have affirmed their respect for the ability of

a dedicated but easy-going colleague. Cyril Lello is well-remembered by two life-long Everton supporters. Kevin Gallagher from Wallasey, and Albert Wilcock from Ness on the Wirral, who as a toddler on his father's shoulders saw the Everton team of 1933 parade the FA Cup through Liverpool. Both recall that he was a ninety minute player, one of the most consistent of his generation. Terry Tyler, an Arsenal supporter from Essex, saw him play at Highbury early in 1956 and recalls *'it soon became obvious that the player who was by far the best player on the pitch was a wing-half. His name screamed at me from the programme. It was Lello. He was everywhere, at once linking defence with attack, back-tracking to help the defence and constantly pushing forward. What a player he was! By half-time the whole East Stand had one man's name on their lips'*. After the ball had been put into touch when an Arsenal player was injured he threw it back to his opponents, a gesture less common in the 1950s than it is now, and half of those in the stand stood up to applaud his sportsmanship. Terry Tyler, then a schoolboy, could not understand why such a gifted footballer did not play for Arsenal.

Cyril Lello's schoolfriend Alf Pilson, photographed when he was in his seventies.

It is fitting that the final tribute to Cyril Lello should come from an opponent. Frank Griffin was a winger who signed for Shrewsbury Town in 1949, two years after Cyril's departure for Everton. He played against Scunthorpe in the club's first game in the Football League in 1950, and was transferred to West Bromwich Albion in the First Division the following year. He gained an FA Cup winner's medal in 1954 when he scored the goal that gave the Albion their 3-2 victory over Preston North End, a game that was watched by Cyril Lello and his Everton colleagues. Frank played against Cyril Lello on several occasions, including a home fixture at The Hawthorns in September 1954, only months after the Cup Final, when the Albion were fourth in Division One and Everton seventh. As a winger Frank respected Cyril's defensive abilities *'After the game was over he was a nice chap, but when you met on the field he was not. He was a good half-back, but he was a hard player. He wasn't very tall, but he was broad and sturdy. If he caught you off balance you went down. If he tackled you, after you picked yourself up, you knew you had been tackled'*. He was eight years younger than Cyril and recalls that his bursts of speed enabled him to sweep past his opponent on several occasions, but that Cyril, unlike some defenders, never bore a grudge after a match.

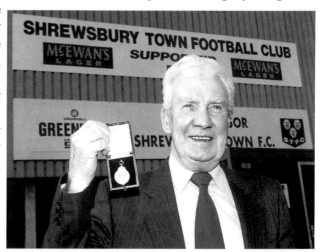

Frank Griffin holding his FA Cup winner's medal of 1954 while re-visiting the Gay Meadow in 1994.

The story of Cyril Lello illustrates much about the history of football, when to play the game as a professional was to follow a working class occupation, which for a limited time provided a glamourous life style, but in other respects was not so very different from being a plumber, a carpenter, a motor mechanic or a compositor. It also shows much about the social history of the twentieth century, about aspects of growing up in a small, traditional urban community, and about the social revolution brought about by World War II. It is also the story of an individual, of one who did not record for posterity his experiences of life, and who might have been surprised that they should be considered interesting. This book has been based on newspaper reports and reminiscences which provide a remarkably unanimous impression of a footballer who was talented, but modest, who regarded football as a craft, and considered that he had a craftsman's responsibility to do a good job, who looked with affection on the town in which he was born and developed his skills, but to which he had no wish to return. He exercised his talents at the highest level, and for a craftsman there can be no greater ambition.

Nil satis, nisi optimum

BIBLIOGRAPHY

Books and articles

Bardsley, C W, *Dictionary of English and Welsh Surnames* (1980), London; Heraldry Today.

Bell, T, *On the Ball City! An illustrated history of Norwich City Football Club* (1972), Norwich: Wensum.

Butler, B, *The Football League 1888-1988* (1987), London: Macdonald.

Collett, M, *The Guinness Record of the FA Cup* (1988), London: Guinness.

Davage, M, *Glorious Canaries Past and Present 1902-1994* (1995), Norwich: Norwich City Football Club.

France, D H, *Toffee Pages: the post-war years* (1997), Witham: Skript.

Hayes, D, *The Goodison Park Encyclopaedia: an A-Z of Everton FC* (1998), London: Mainstream.

Inglis, S, *The Football Grounds of England and Wales* (1985), London: Willow.

Jones, C, 'Electricity Supply in Shropshire before Nationalisation', *Industrial Archaeology Review, vol. 18* (1996), 201-22.

Jones, M, '*Breath on 'em Salop: Shrewsbury Town FC: The Official History* (1995), Harefield: Yore Publications.

Kelly, *Directories of Shropshire* (1905, 1926, 1937)

Lloyd, D J, *A short history of St Laurence's Church of England Infants School, Ludlow and its predecessors 1847-1991* (1991), Ludlow: privately published.

Lloyd, D, J, *The Concise History of Ludlow* (1999), Ludlow: Merlin Unwin.

Morgan, T J, & Morgan, P, *Welsh Surnames* (1985), Cardiff: University of Wales Press.

Nannestad, I, & Nannestad, D, *Lincoln City FC: the Official History* (nd), Harefield: Yore Publications.

Oliver, K M, *Through Adversity: the History of the RAF Regiment 1942-1992* (1997), Rushden: Forces & Corporate.

Roberts, J, *Everton – the Official Centenary History* (1978), Manchester: Granada.

Rollin, J, *Soccer at War 1939-45* (1985), London: Willow.

Ross, I & Smailes, G, *Everton: a complete record* (1993), Derby: Breedon.

Trinder, B, *A History of Shropshire* (second edition, 1998), Chichester: Phillimore.

Turner, D, & White, A, *The Breedon Book of Football Managers* (1993), Derby: Breedon.

Walvin, J, *The People's Game: the social history of British Football* (1975), London: Allen Lane.

Newspapers

Daily Herald
Daily Sketch
Empire News
Evening Express
Express and Star
Hereford Times
Lincolnshire Echo
Liverpool Echo

Ludlow Advertiser
Ludlow Standard
Rochdale Observer
Runcorn Weekly News
Shrewsbury Chronicle
Sunday Chronicle
Wellington Journal

Other sources

Everton FC match programmes with significant data concerning Cyril Lello:
v Newcastle United 24 January 1970
v Arsenal 1 March 1997
v Manchester United 27 August 1997.

Charles Buchan's Football Monthly, No 31 (March 1954), pp. 30-31, 'Spotlight on Everton'; No 54 (February 1956), p. 27, 'Cyril Lello, Everton, "I was taken for a ride".

The Broad Gate, magazine of Ludlow Senior School.

Voters' registers for Ludlow (Shropshire Records & Research).

RAF Servicemen's Records, RAF Personnel & Training Command, RAF Innsworth, Gloucester.

Web sites:

Derry City FC. http://www.derrycityfc.com
Everton FC. http://evertonfc.merseyworld.com
Rochdale FC. www.rochdale-football-club.co.uk

INDEX

Aalborg, ...46
Aberdeen FC, .46
Accrington Stanley FC, ...56
Acton, Frank, ...22,23
Adams, Jack, .17
Alamein, battle, ...32
Allchurch, Ivor, ...48
Angell, Leslie, ...16
Anzio, battle, .32
Arhus, ...46
Arrowsmith, Ernest, ...22,23
Arsenal FC, ...34,48,39,52,67,68
Assam, ...32
Aston Villa FC, ...31,41,43,51,54,65
Atyeo, John 49
Augsburg, ...46
Austria, ...46

Badlan:
      Bill, ...33,40,66
      H, ...24,25
      Rachel, .66
Ball, Alan, ...41
Bangor City FC, ...25,59
Banks,
      Alfred .26
      Bradney, ...22,23,26
Barry Town FC, ...30
Bartram, Sam, ...51
Belgium, ...32,33
Belton Park, Lincs., ...33
Binns, Eric, ...57
Birch, K, ...53,54
Birmingham, ...15,20,28,42
Birmingham City FC, ...30,31,37,41,48
Bishop's Castle, Shropshire, ...30
Bithell,-, ...19
Bitterley, Shropshire, ...17,18
Blackburn Rovers FC, ...57
Blackpool, ...33
Blackpool FC, ...43

Black Swan, HMS, sloop, ...32
Blanchflower, Danny, ...51,55
Bodenham, John, ...22,23,33
Bolton Wanderers FC, ...43
Bootle Cricket Club, ...47
Borth, Dyfed, .32
Boston United FC 29,37
Boulton, - 24
Boxing, ...18
Bradford (Park Avenue) FC, ...38
Bradford City FC, ...31,37
Brampton Bryan, Herefs., ...46
Brazil 53
Bridgnorth, Shropshire, ...17
Brighton, .43,44
Bristol City FC 53
Britton, Cliff, ...33,43,44,49,53
Broadbent, Peter, ...50
Broadis, Ivor, .54
Bromfield, Shropshire, ...23
Broome, Frank, ...33
Brown, Alan, ...18,23,26
Brunton, Jack, ...25
Buchan, Ian, ...53,54
Bucknell, Shropshire 30,67
Bucknell FC, .28
Burma, ...31
Burton, -, ...17
Burton, Deany, ...22,49
Bury FC, ...43,48,56
Butlin, Billy, .33
Buxton, Derby 44,45
Buxton FC 59

Cadwalleder, C, ...25
Campbell, -, .26
Canada, ...46
Cardiff City FC, ...42
Carter, John, .63
Cartwright, Frank, ...22,25

Catterick, Harry, ...39,40,54,56,57,61,62
Celle, Germany, ...36
Celtic FC, ...37
Charity football competitions, ...29
Charlton, -, ...24
Charlton Athletic FC, ...51
Chatham, Kent, ...32
Cheadle, V, ...24
Chelmsford, Essex, ...30
Chelsea FC, ...37,39,50,51
Cheltenham Town FC, ...31
Chester, ...18
Chester City FC, ...56,57
Church Stretton, Shropshire, ...24,26,27,30
Church Stretton FC, ...26
Clark, George, ...22,28
Clee Hill FC, ...22,29
Clee Hills 12,22,23,31
Clegg, A R, ...16
Cleobury Mortimer, Shropshire, ...47
Clinton, Tommy, ...43,44,57,58,63,67
Collier:
      Artie 18,28
      Jack 18,19,28,33
Cologne, ...46
Coningsby, Lincs., ...35
Cooper:
      G, ...28
      Hugo, ...26
      Tony, ...22,23
Copenhagen, ...46
Coventry City FC, ...30,31
Craven Arms, Shropshire, . . .17,18,25,29,30
Creswell, H, ...28
Crewe Alexander FC, ...56
Cricket 22,44,47
Crump, Ben, ...33
Cullis, Stan, ...31
Cunningham, Willy, ...50,59

Daines, Edward, ...34,67
Darts, ...63
Davies:
      Cyril, ...21,22,23

CT, ...24,25
      Henry 26
      Jack, ...22,23
      Leonard, ...26,28
      Mary (née Pilson), ...23
      'Togger', ...25
      Tom 24,25
      William 25
Denaby United FC, ...37,38
Denmark, ...46
Derby County FC, ...35,48
Derry City FC, ...37
Dickinson, Jimmy, ...55
Disley, A, ...26
Docherty, Tommy, ...49,50,55
Dodd, -, ...21
Doddington, Shropshire, ...30
Dolphins, Cricket Club, ...46,47,66
Doncaster Rovers FC, ...35,42
Dorset, ...33,42
Dugdale, Gordon, ...63,64
Dunkirk, ...31
Dunn, Jimmy, .57
Dyer, Percy, ...26

Eastern Daily Press 34
Eden, Teddy, ...30,31
Edwards:
      Duncan, ...50,56
      Jasper, ...27,28
      Ken, ...28
      Sydney, ...26
Eglington, Tommy, ...39,40,42,43,47,48
Elan Valley aqueduct, ...28
Esbjerg, ...46
Evans, A E, ...16
Everall:
      Don, ...65,66
      W, ...26
Everton FC:
  cricket teams, ...47
  Cyril Lello's continuing links with, 10,62,63
  half-back line: Farrell, Jones, Lello,41,50,51,54
  half-back line: Harvey, Kendall, Ball, ...41

history before World War II, ...39
managed by Harry Catterick, ...61,62
owns houses in Goodison Avenue, . . .10,62
promotion to Division One, ...48,49,65
relegation to Division Two, ...42
season 1946-47 39
season 1947-48, ...40
season 1948-49, ...41
season 1949-50, ...41
season 1951-52, ...42
season 1952-53, ...43
season 1953-54 47,48,66
season 1954-55, ...49,50
season 1955-56, ...51,52,53
season 1956-57, ...54
season 1984-85, ...62
signing of Cyril Lello, ...39
transfers of leading players 1945-46, ...39

Falkirk FC, ...34
Farrell, Peter, ...39-43,47-54
Fielding, Wally 40,41,50
Fields, Gracie, ...56
Filey, Yorks, ...33
Finney, Tom, ...10,49,50,55
Flint Town FC, ...58
Follows, George, ...51
Franklin, Neil, ...10
Freeman, 'Bandy', ...22
French, John, ...25
Fulham FC, ...61
Furlong:
      James, ...44
      Millie (née Healey), ...44

Gallagher, Kevin, ...64
Gateshead United FC, ...32,52
Gazey,-, ...24
Germany, ...6,10,31,32,36,46
Golf, ...43,67
Gloucester City FC, ...30
Gough, J, .26,28
Grant, Jackie, ...40,42,56,58,63,64
Grantham FC, ...38,39

Green, James, ...12
Greenhalgh, Norman, ...39,63,64
Griffin, Frank, ...48,68
Grimsby Town FC, ...35

Haley, Bill, ...56
Hancocks, Johnny, ...40,58
Hanwood, Shropshire, ...38,54
Hanwood Colliery FC, ...29
Hapgood, Eddie, ...34,38
Harrogate, ...43,44
Harvey, Joe, ...45
Harwich, Essex, ...46
Haverfordwest, Pembs., ...36
Heath, Fred, ...49
Hereford, .12,32
Hereford Times, ...31
Hereford United FC, ...25,30,31,63
Hickson, Dave, ...43,48-51,63-65,67
Hobbs, Clifford, ...21
Hodder, Bill, ...59
Hodges, family, ...13
Hookagate United FC, ...27,28,33
Hopton Swifts FC, ...29
Houghton, Eric, ...31
Houseman, J, ...28
Howells, Bill, ...24,25
Hughes, Arthur, ...38,65,67
Hull City FC, ...43
Hullett, Billy, ...35
Hungary, .50,54
Hunter:
      Robert, ...26,27
      Dr Thomas, ...16,19
Hyde FC, ...58
India 22
Ipswich 34
Ironbridge, Shropshire, ...40
Italy 32,33

Jeffs: Bill, ...33
       Harvey, ...33
Jones
      C, ...24

Dennis, ...25
Tommy, ...39-40,48-50
W, ...24

Keeling, -, .25
Keenan, -, .31
Kelly, Theo, ...39,41,44
Kendall, Don, ...44
Kendall, Howard, ...41,62
Kershaw, E G, ...63
Key, E, ...26
Keyse, G, ...25
Kidderminster Harriers FC, ...29
King's Norton, Warwicks., ...18
King's Shropshire Light Infantry, ...13
Kirkdale, Lancs., ...44
Knighton, Leslie, ...39
Knighton, Rads., ...28,30,46
Knowbury, Shropshire, ...24,30
Korean War 63

Laver, Jim, ...22,23,29,30,48
Lawton:
    Fred .29
    Tommy, ...39,65
Leach, Sam, ...29
Leeds United FC, ...43,54
Lee Beesley Ltd., ...61
Leicester City FC, ...42
Leintwardine, Herefs., ...34
Lello: origins of name, ...12
Lello:
    Clara Jane (née Preece), ...12-15
    Cyril Francis (b 1954), ...14,44,45,62
    Cyril Francis (b 1979), ...14,62
    Cyril Frank (1920-97),
        acquires motor car, ...57
        changes position to wing-half, ...41
        characteristics as footballer, . . .10,11,18,
       35,37,40,47,54,65,67,68
        childhood, ...10,12,13,45
        coaches church youth team, ...62
        continuing links with Everton, .10,62,63
        education, ...14-19,65

employment at Lee Beesley, ...61
girl friends, ...19
home in Goodison Avenue 44,45,56,
. 57,59,62,64,67
illness and death, ...10,64
injury 1950-52, ...41,42,48
interest in fishing, ...45
interest in woodwork, ...17,45
lack of international recognition, . .18,55
links with Ludlow, .40,46,49,62,63,65,66
plays football for:
    Boys' Brigade, ...20-21
    Derry City, ...34,35
    Early Closers, ...22-23
    Everton, ...39-55
    Hereford United, ...25,30,31,63
    Lincoln City, ...35,36,63
    Ludford Amateurs, ...23
    Ludlow Town, ...27-28
    Millwall, ...36
    New Brighton. 59,60
    North of Ireland, ...35
    Norwich City, ...34
    Rochdale, ...54,56,57
    Runcorn, ...54,57,59
    school, ...17-18
    Shrewsbury Town, 17,29,30,37-39,63,65
    Try-Hards, ...21-22
RAF career 31-36,46,55,63,66,67
retirement from professional football,1,61
Elsie (née Healey), ...14,43,44,45,62
Gertrude Ellen (Nellie), ...9,10,58
Harold George, ...10,11,14-16,18,20-23,
. 31-33,35,36,44,46,43
Leslie John, ...13,14,16,18,32,44,46,47
Stanley Edward (Ted), ...13,14,16,29
Thomas Henry, ...10,11-15,46,58
Winifred Elsie, ...13,14,16
Leominster, Herefs., ...20
Lincoln City FC, ...35-38
Liverpool, ...44,45,48,56,59,61,62
Liverpool Echo, ...17,45,46
Liverpool FC, ...40,41,44,59,67
Llandridnod Wells, Powys, ...31

Lloyd, Joe, ...24
Lofthouse, Nat, ...10,43,55
Loughrane, Fr Matthew, ...62
Ludford, ...8
Ludford Amateurs FC, ...18,21,23-27,30,32
Ludlow:
    Angel Hotel, .29
    Boys's Brigade, ...20-21
    building trade, ...20
    castle, ...12,20
    casualties in World War 1, ...13
    casualties in World War 2, ...33
    characteristics in 1930s, .18,20,32,65-67
    cricket, ...see Dolphins CC
    Cosy Corner, ...63
    dances, ...29
    darts, ...63
    Dinham, . .12,13,15,16,36,47,54,62,63,65
    electricity supply, ...13,46
    Feathers Hotel, ...25
    football clubs, see Ludford Amateurs FC,
    . . . . .Ludlow Early Closers FC,
    . . . . .Ludlow Town FC,
    . . . . .Try Hards FC,
    Galdeford, ...13,16,17,20,21,46
    geology, ...12
    hospitals, ...16
    Linney, ...16
    Portcullis Lane, ...13
    Pitt & Minton Cup, ...63
    reputation of Cyril Lello, .40,41,44,48,50
   62,63,67
    Sandpits Road, ...17,18,20
    schools .16,22
    soup kitchen, ...20
    St Lawrence church, ...12,13
    St Stephen's Hall 20,21,29
    Star & Garter inn, ...50
    Steventon, .52
    Tinkers' Hill, ...12
    visitors' impressions of, ...12
    whist drives, ...29
    Whitcliffe, ...12,13,16

Ludlow Advertiser, ...17,18,21,22,43,63
Ludlow Early Closers FC, ...22,23,29,30,33
Ludlow Standard, ...22,29
Ludlow Town FC 23-27,33,65
Luton Town FC, ...34
Lydbury North, Shropshire, ...30

Machine Gun Corps, ...13
McClelland, Joe, ...36
Manchester, ...32,42,43
Manchester City FC, ...37,41,50,51,64
Manchester United FC,31,35,43,50,54,62,64,67
Mannion, Wilf, .40
Mansfield Town FC, ...35
Mapp, Wilfred, ...22,23
Marchi, Tony, ...51
Marston:
    Bill 21
    Clifford, ...17
    Jack, ...17
Matthews:
    Bill 26
    Stanley, ...10,43,54,55,65
Maximum wage, ...10,45,61,62
Mercer, Joe, ...31,39,63,64
Merrick, Gil, ...10,48
Middlesbrough FC, ...34,40,41
Milbourne, F, .28
Millwall FC, ...36
Minton, Gordon 63
Monmouth, ...31
Mossley FC, ...58
Munich, ...50
Murmansk 32

Nash:
    Bill, ...16,18-20,25,26,32,51,54,63
    Esmée, ...32
Nason, Billy, ...23,33
Netherlands, ...32,46
Newark, Notts., ...37
New Brighton FC, ...59-61
Newcastle United FC, ...33
Nicholas, Ben, ...20,26,29,32

Normandy, landings and battle, ...32,35
Northern Ireland, ...34,35
Northwich Victoria FC, ...59
Norwich, ...34
Norwich City FC, ...34,36
Nottingham Forest FC, ...30,35,43
Notts County FC, ...35,42,63

Oakengates, Shropshire, ...40
Oaks, Paddy, ...26
Oakley Park, Shropshire, ...21
Oldham Athletic FC, ...47,48
O'Neill, Jimmy, ...43,45,50
Oswestry Town FC, ...25,29,58

Padfield, Bessie, ...16
Page, Ernest, ...63
Parker, John Willie, ...40,41,45,48-51,56
Parsonage, Wilfred, ...29
Partick Thistle FC, ...37
Pearce, Wallace, ...25
Pendlebury, W H, ...16
Penny Lane, Liverpoool, ...61
Perry, P.S.H. 17
Peterborough United FC, ...33
Pilson, Alf, . . .16,18-19,29,32,33,42,43,67,68
Pinches, George, ...26
Pitt, Denis, ...59
Plymouth Argyll FC, ...43,48
Pontesbury FC, ...38
Portlock:
        George, ...16
        Gerald, ...16
        William, .16
Portsmouth FC, ...40,51,55
Port Vale FC, ...30,53
Potts, Jack, ...24
Powell, Wallace, ...22,23
Powis:
        Arthur, ...15,27,29
        Charles, ...26,27
        Jack, ...17,29,33
        William, ...27,29
Pratt, William, ...26

Preece, Mary Ellen, ...12
Prescot Cables FC, ...57,59
Presteign, Rads., ...30
Preston North End FC, ...30,49-51,68
Pritchard, George, ...33
Pudleston, Herefs., ...12

Queen Elizabeth, RMS, ...46
Quigley, Eddie, ...58

Ramsey, Alf, ...10
Ransomes & Marles FC, ...37
Ratcliffe, Kevin, ...62
Reading, G, ...28
Reading FC 34
Reid, Peter, ...62
Revie, Don, .50,51
Reynolds, Jack, ...17,18,21,23,54,56
Richards:
        Alfred, ...26,27
        Arthur, ...26,27
        Len, .26,27
Robbins, Bill, ...24,25
Roberts, -, ...26
Robinson, -, ...25
Robledo, George, ...54
Rochdale, ...56
Rochdale FC, ...54,56,57,67
Rochdale Observer, ...56
Rogers, Sam, ...54,66
Rotherham United FC, ...35
Rowley, Jack, ...31,35,50
Royal Air Force, ...6,27
Royal Air Force Regiment, ...31-36,46
Royal Navy 32
Royle, Joe, ...53
Runcorn FC, ...54,57-59,61,67
Runcorn Weekly News, ...57,59

Sagar, Ted, ...39,40,42,63,64
Salzburg, ...46
Scarborough United FC, ...37,38
Scheveningen, .46
Schweinfurt, ...42

Scott, Jack, ...22,23
Scunthorpe United FC, ...6,67
Seabury, A, ...26
Sexton, Dave, ...55
Seymour, Tommy, ...38
Shackleton, Len, ...10,50,54,55
Shamrock Rovers FC, ...39
Shaw, Lancs., ...56
Sheffield United FC, ...35,49
Sheffield Wednesday FC, ...22,31,50
Sheldon, H, .24
Shifnal, Shrops., ...29
Shrewsbury, ...12,18,22,32
Shrewsbury Chronicle, ...22,23,25,29,37
Shrewsbury Town FC, ...27,29-31,33,34,
. 36-39,44,48,54,63,65-68
Shrops, Worcs & Staffs Electricity Co., .13,46
Silsden, Yorks., ...36
Singapore, ...33
Small, Edward Leslie, ...23,24,29
Smith, Gaius, ...22
Southall, Neville, ...53,62
Southampton, ...42,46
Southampton FC, ...34,46
Southend United FC, ...34
Southport FC, ...56
Stafford Rangers FC, ...25,59
Stanbridge, Beds., ...34
Starling, Ron, ...31
Steel, Len, ...24
Stephens, W S, ...22
Stevenson, Alex, ...39,63,64
Stockport County FC, ...56,58
Stoke City FC, ...41
Sunderland, FC, ...50
Swansea City FC, ...42,48
Sweden, ...44
Swift, Frank, ...10

Tansey, Jimmy, ...45
Taylor, Charles 25,26
Telford, Thomas, ...12
Tipton:
    Denis, ...22,26

    Gordon, ...22,28,49
    Jack, ...22
Titley:
    Charles, ...26,27
    Eric, ...27
    John, ...27,28
Torquay United FC, ...25
Tottenham Hotspur FC, ...41,51,52
Tranmere Rovers FC, ...59
Trautmann, Bert, ...10
Try Hards FC 21,22,29
Tudor, A, ...26
Turner:
    J M W, ...12
    T.L. 57
Tyler, Terry, ...52,68

United States of America, ...46

Vancouver, ...46,47
Viollet, Denis, ...50,55
Vow, E, ...26

Wainwright, Eddie, ...45,50
Walsall FC, .44
Watford FC, .34
Watkins, L, .28
Watson, Gordon, ...39,63,64
Wellington Town FC, ...37,48
West Bromwich Albion FC, ...30,48,68
West Ham United FC, ...34,50
Wheeler, John, ...17
Williams,
    Gordon, ...26
    L, ...24
    W R, ...39
    -, ...26
Williamson, -, ...22
Widnes, 59
Wilcock, Albert, ...68
Winsford FC, ...58-60
Wistanstow, Shrops., ...19
Wolverhampton, ...18,41
Wolverhampton Wanderers FC, .29,35,37,39,

. 40,50,57,58,66
Worcester City FC, ...29
Workington FC, ...59
World War I, ...10,11,66
World War II, ...10,17,
. 29-36,66,68
Wrexham FC, ...56,59
Wunstorf, Gemany, ...36
Wright, Billy, ...10,40,50,55

Yapp, S, ...28
Yates, Jack, ...25
Yeovill Town FC, ...27